S0-ADT-153

CREATING YOUR
High School Portfolio

An Interactive Guide for Documenting and Planning Your Education, Career, and Life

SECOND EDITION

✐ Create a portfolio that documents your skills and values and describes what you have done and what you can do

✐ Learn how to choose your career direction and assess your progress

✐ Plan your approach to getting more education and training

✐ Chart your course for getting a job

By the Editors at JIST

JIST Works

Creating Your High School Portfolio, *Second Edition*

An Interactive Guide for Documenting and Planning Your Education, Career, and Life

© 2003 by JIST Publishing

Published by JIST Works, an imprint of JIST Publishing
7321 Shadeland Station, Suite 200
Indianapolis, IN 46256-3923

Phone: 800-648-JIST   Fax: 877-454-7839
E-mail: info@jist.com   Web site: www.jist.com

Note to instructors. This workbook *(Creating Your High School Portfolio)* is part of a curriculum that also includes a resume-writing workbook *(Creating Your High School Resume)* and an instructor's guide. The instructor's guide covers both workbooks. The workbooks can be used separately or together, depending on your class objectives. All materials are available separately from JIST.

Videos on portfolio development, resumes, and job search topics are also available from JIST. The Web site offers information at free and subscription levels. Call 800-648-JIST for details.

Quantity discounts are available for JIST products. Have future editions of JIST books automatically delivered to you on publication through our convenient standing order program. Please call 800-648-JIST or visit www.jist.com for a free catalog and more information.

Visit www.jist.com. Find out about our products, order a catalog, and link to other career-related sites. You can also learn more about JIST authors and JIST training available to professionals.

Acquisitions Editor: Susan Pines
Contributing Writer: Judit E. Price
Development Editor: Veda Dickerson
Cover and Interior Designer: Aleata Howard
Page Layout Coordinator: Carolyn J. Newland
Proofreaders: Stephanie Koutek, Jeanne Clark
Indexer: Jeanne Clark

Acknowledgment: The first and second JIST Publishing editions of this book are a complete revision of an earlier work titled *Life Work Portfolio*. The work was a joint project of the National Occupational Information Coordinating Committee (NOICC), the Maine Occupational Information Coordinating Committee, and the Career Development Training Institute at Oakland University. It was developed with an advisory committee representing job training, adult education, and displaced homemaker programs and was reviewed by a national review team comprising leaders in the career development field. The book was also pilot-tested at major universities, corporate sites, veterans affairs offices, job training programs, and community colleges. While the JIST Publishing editions incorporate major changes, they would not have been possible without the effort of the many people involved in the original *Life Work Portfolio* project.

Printed in the United States of America

09 08 07   9 8 7 6 5 4

All rights reserved. No part of this book may be reproduced in any form or by any means, or stored in a database or retrieval system, without prior permission of the publisher except in the case of brief quotations embodied in articles or reviews. Making copies of any part of this book for any purpose other than your own personal use is a violation of United States copyright laws. For permission requests, please contact the Copyright Clearance Center at www.copyright.com or (978) 750-8400.

We have been careful to provide accurate information throughout this book, but it is possible that errors and omissions have been introduced. Please consider this in making any career plans or other important decisions. Trust your own judgment above all else and in all things.

Trademarks: All brand names and product names used in this book are trade names, service marks, trademarks, or registered trademarks of their respective owners.

ISBN 978-1-56370-906-7

About This Book

A portfolio is a collection of records that document your education and work history. A portfolio affirms your successes. *Creating Your High School Portfolio* is a unique workbook that explains the practical side of portfolio creation and takes you step-by-step through education and career planning. The pages are perforated and three-hole punched, so you can easily add completed worksheets to your portfolio as desired.

Creating Your High School Portfolio shows you how to collect and present the documents you need when applying for jobs, for college, or for training programs. It also introduces the steps of career decision making. As you gain experience or your situation changes, you will be able to use this process more than once.

You are always growing and maturing, and the job market is always changing. This means you will probably change your job or career several times throughout your life. *Creating Your High School Portfolio* shows you how to update your portfolio to reflect the changes in your life. Your portfolio is an ongoing record of your achievements, skills, experiences, and goals.

Creating Your High School Portfolio shows you how to research schools and careers, explore your options, and set goals. Take time to reflect on yourself, your interests, your achievements, and your dreams. It may take a day, a week, or a month to gather and arrange the documents that detail your life, education, and career. But it will be a worthwhile investment in your future.

Table of Contents

Introduction

As a high school student, you consider many education and career options. *Creating Your High School Portfolio* encourages you to approach your life with confidence and describes how to create, organize, and use a portfolio.

Portfolios are not just for artists or for adults. You, too, can benefit from having a portfolio. This updated version of *Creating Your High School Portfolio* provides you with valuable resources:

- Suggestions about what to include in your portfolio and how to organize and use it

- Worksheets for understanding your career and life values, your learning and personality styles, your self-management style, and your changing life roles

- Ideas for creating an electronic portfolio

- A plan for making career and education decisions

This book provides numerous worksheets that guide you in making good decisions. The pages are perforated and three-hole punched, so you can easily remove them if you choose. Complete each worksheet. You may want to put completed worksheets in your portfolio as a reference. Or you can leave the worksheets in the book and keep the workbook handy for reference.

If you get stuck or have questions about creating your portfolio and about making career and education decisions, help is available in many forms. The best place to start, of course, is with your school guidance office. You can also consult people who work in careers that interest you. Talk to your teachers. Check out the Internet, beginning with www.jist.com. Talk to your parents, your friends, and your mentor.

Congratulations on deciding to complete this workbook. Your preparation greatly increases your chance of finding success in your life and career!

Part One

Creating a Portfolio

Chapter 1

Introduction to Portfolios

Welcome to the world of portfolios! You may not know anything about portfolios. Or you may already know about portfolios but just need some help. You may even have a portfolio but want to improve it. This chapter helps answer these questions:

- What is a portfolio?
- Can a portfolio help me?
- Why do I need to know what my goals are?
- What should I put in my portfolio?
- What are some options for organizing my portfolio?
- What should I keep my portfolio in?
- Can I use my portfolio in interviews?

A portfolio is a tool that can help you succeed. Hopefully, as you create your portfolio, you will be inspired to build on your skills and to take charge of your education and career.

Definition of a Portfolio

Portfolios are not new. People such as artists and teachers have used portfolios for a long time. Today, people in almost all careers use portfolios. As a high school student, you too can use a portfolio.

You probably already know what a resume is, and your resume should be part of your portfolio. But a portfolio is not the same thing as a resume. The following chart shows some of the differences.

> People in almost all careers use portfolios. As a high school student, you too can use a portfolio.

Resume	Portfolio
Student resumes are usually just one page.	Portfolios are made up of a group of documents.
A resume is a summary of what you've done, what you've learned, and what you are interested in.	A portfolio contains documents that prove what you say in your resume.
Your resume might say that you like to help other people.	Your portfolio might contain a letter from your teacher thanking you for spending time with a new student.

You will use your portfolio when you are interviewing for college or trade school admission. You also will use these documents when you are applying for a job. The documents in your portfolio show

- What you have accomplished
- What your skills are
- What experiences you have had
- What you have done to improve yourself
- What your goals and values are
- What you know
- What your school and career preferences are

When you are a freshman or sophomore in high school, you will use your portfolio mainly to get to know yourself better. It will be an important learning tool for you.

In your junior and senior years, you will actually begin to use your portfolio in interviews. It will help you as you make decisions about your education and career goals.

When you finish school, you will use your portfolio as a tool for marketing yourself to potential employers. Or you may use it when you meet with college admissions personnel.

My Definition

Here's my definition of a portfolio.

_____

_____

_____

Benefits of a Portfolio

A portfolio helps you evaluate yourself and your progress. Portfolios are important because

- Your grades do not show everything about you

- Your grades do not show what you are capable of understanding

- Your grades do not show what you are capable of doing

- Your grades do not show what activities you are involved in when you are not in school

> Putting together a portfolio lets you see what is good about you. It lets you see how you have grown and what you have done.

Imagine how things were when your parents and grandparents got out of school. They probably planned to get a job and stay at the same company for many years. And they may have done just that.

Today, things are different. You are affected by events in other parts of the world. The American economy and job market are always changing. You may have several jobs during your life. You will need to be able to

- Find a new job

- Learn new skills

- Find new ways to use the skills you already have

Have you heard the word *self-direction?* It means that **you** are in control of your future. You must be able to present yourself well to admissions officers and employers.

When you are talking to an interviewer, that person knows little or nothing about you. You have to paint a picture of yourself that is positive and true. Your portfolio helps you do this. You can use your portfolio to get accepted into college or into a training program. You can use it for finding any kind of job you are interested in.

And here's something you may not have thought about: Putting together your portfolio will build your self-confidence. Do you usually overlook what you have accomplished? Do you tend to emphasize the things you aren't good at? If so, you are like most people. Putting together a portfolio lets you see what is good about you. It lets you see how you have grown and what you have done.

Have you ever really examined yourself? Do you know who you are? Do you know what you want in life? If you do, you will be able to set and achieve your goals. You can learn a lot about yourself by getting together the information for your portfolio.

Be Ready—Things Change

The world changes rapidly. All of us are affected. But you can deal with change if you expect it and know how to recognize it. Your portfolio shows how your life has already changed. It helps you make decisions about your education and career. It shows you that you are not helpless.

> Your portfolio shows how your life has already changed. It shows you that you are not helpless.

Your portfolio includes specific examples of how you have changed and grown. It's a tool that helps you present yourself to interviewers.

Think about how your life may change in the future. Remember this: Learning should not end when you graduate from school. You can keep learning throughout your life. In fact, what you are really being taught in high school is how to learn. You are learning the skills you will need to continue to change and grow.

Look at Yourself and Your Skills

College admissions officers, guidance counselors, and employers love portfolios. Why? Because a portfolio is objective. It tells an interviewer what other people think about you. It includes

- Reference letters
- Certificates of achievement
- School awards
- Newspaper or magazine articles showing what you have done in your community
- Thank-you letters from people you have helped

> You can use your portfolio to help your teachers and counselors know you better. The more they know about you, the better the advice they will be able to give you.

Each item in your portfolio is evidence of your skills, knowledge, and values. These characteristics define who you are and what kind of student or employee you will be. You can use these and other documents to impress interviewers. Creating a positive first impression is important when you are

- Getting ready to graduate from high school
- Looking for a job
- Applying for acceptance into college or some other training program

You know what you have experienced and what you have achieved. You know that you are mature and committed. And you know that these are qualities interviewers look for. Still, you may have a hard time describing how everything fits together. Your portfolio gives you a way to tell an interviewer about your skills and experiences.

The advice of your teachers and guidance counselors is important to your success. But your high school classes are probably large, and your teachers and counselors are very busy. You can use your portfolio to help your teachers and counselors know you better. The more they know about you, the better the advice they will be able to give you.

Show How You've Progressed

 A portfolio is not put together randomly. It should be organized in a way that clearly shows the steps you have taken to reach your goals.

A portfolio is not put together randomly. It should be organized in a way that clearly shows the steps you have taken to reach your goals.

Imagine that you are showing someone your portfolio. You should be able to tell the person what each piece of information represents. You should be able to describe how you have grown as a person, student, and employee.

You do not have to organize your portfolio in date order. For example, you might start with a section on education and training. Then you might continue with a section on your accomplishments and job history. Next, you might have a section that shows your skills and attributes. You might follow that with a section that illustrates your values, and so forth.

The point is that you can organize your portfolio any way you want. But be sure you can explain why you organized it a certain way.

I Benefit

Here's a short description of one way I think a portfolio would benefit me.

_____

_____

_____

Portfolios and Goal-Setting

You may have a difficult time reaching some of the goals you set as a student. But just setting goals may give you the courage to try to achieve those goals.

The following ideas will help you reach your goals:

- Set goals that are specific.
- Set goals you can reach.
- Set goals you can measure.
- Set goals that are realistic.
- Set a deadline for each step you will take toward reaching your goals.
- Set some long-range goals—ones you will reach sometime in the future.
- Set some short-range goals—ones you will reach soon.

> Setting goals may give you the courage to try to achieve those goals.

You may also want to set some goals that can never be reached. These are goals that give your life direction. For example, you might choose one of these goals:

- To always keep learning, even when you are no longer a student
- To be number one in your career
- To be the best you can be

You will not always have an easy time reaching your goals. Certain obstacles and circumstances may force you to reevaluate your goals. This is not necessarily bad. These barriers can help you grow.

Be sure to set some goals before you create your portfolio. If you do, you'll be able to

- See what you need to do to reach your goals
- Identify things that might keep you from reaching your goals
- Think about ways to deal with those things

Your goals determine what you should include in your portfolio.

Before you can set goals, you must know

- What your strengths and weaknesses are
- What your values are
- What you want from your career
- What your skills and abilities are
- What you want to accomplish

When you know these things, you can set realistic goals. You will learn more about setting goals in Part Three of this book.

One Goal

Here's one example of a goal a high school student might have. _____

_____

_____

Student Portfolios

Most interviewers—from college recruiters to restaurant managers—know what type person they are looking for. They don't have time to hear everything about your life or school activities. But they do want information that helps them make a final decision. Show them examples from your portfolio that are clear, relevant, and interesting.

> Most interviewers—from college recruiters to restaurant managers—know what type person they are looking for. Interviewers want information that helps them make a final decision.

As a student, you may want to create a portfolio that emphasizes just one aspect of your life, such as sports, community service, or writing. You can use this kind of portfolio when you apply for internships or for work-study programs. You can also use it when you are first trying to get a job.

You have limited work experience, so you have to let the interviewer know that you have potential. Many interviewers are more interested in quality people than in people who have years of experience. As a student, you might also be able to use a portfolio that is targeted to one specific job or school. Include only the information that relates to that job or school.

The Master Portfolio

 Tip Update your Master Portfolio often. Replace old information with newer and more up-to-date information.

As you get ready to put together a portfolio, think about this:

- You may want to have a Master Portfolio. This is a portfolio that contains every piece of information you have about yourself and your background.

- You would also create portfolios that are subsets of the Master Portfolio. These would include only information that applies to a certain situation.

If you are applying for a job:

- Learn as much as you can about what your job description would be.

- Pull documents out of your Master Portfolio that show that you have the qualities you would need in that job.

For example, if you want a job that involves working on a team, include examples of times when you have worked with other people.

If you are applying for college or some other type of training or schooling:

- Think about what you plan to study.
- Pull information from your Master Portfolio that shows why you are a good candidate for the program you are applying for.

For example, you could pull information that shows what high grades you made or what kind of technical knowledge you have.

Update your Master Portfolio often. Be sure the items you include emphasize your best accomplishments. Replace old information with newer and more up-to-date information.

Organizing Your Portfolio

As you create your first portfolio, you will see that you have more materials than you need. That's good. Get together as much information as you can. Then you can choose the best examples and decide which sections of your portfolio to emphasize. Bits and pieces of information may not say much about you. But when you put everything together, you get a bigger picture of who you are.

> As you create your first portfolio, you will see that you have more materials than you need. That's good. Get together as much information as you can.

Also, remember that a document can serve more than one purpose. For example, if you win an award in your computer science class, you can use the award to show that you have computer experience and that you value your education.

The following paragraphs describe three ways you could organize your portfolio:

- Organize based on your multiple intelligences
- Organize based on your SCANS skills
- Organize based on your self-exploration

This book gives suggestions for the self-exploration method of organization. If you are using this method of organizing your portfolio, these suggestions will apply specifically to you. If you are using the Multiple Intelligences or SCANS Skills method of organizing your portfolio, these suggestions can help you, too. The organization will be different. But you will include the same kind of information no matter how you organize your portfolio.

Multiple Intelligences

Multiple intelligences isn't a phrase you hear everyday. Right? So, what does it mean?

The concept of multiple intelligences was developed by Dr. Howard Gardner, a professor at Harvard University. When people use the term *intelligence* they are usually talking about how smart someone is. When Dr. Gardner uses the term, he is talking about how someone applies his or her intelligence.

Dr. Gardner might say that your intelligence refers to your ability to solve problems. You were born with a certain level of intelligence. It's internal. It can't be changed. You apply your intelligence in various situations.

Here's an example: You start a computer business. You are very good at your job. People say you are intelligent. But when you are expected to make friends, you can't. People do not think of you as intelligent in that area. Or maybe you can do both—use computers and make friends. If so, Dr. Gardner would say you have multiple intelligences.

How does this apply to you? Interviewers are looking for people who can function and solve problems in several types of situations. You want to show them that you are that kind of person. To do this, you could arrange your portfolio around your areas of intelligence.

Dr. Gardner identifies nine kinds of intelligence. You may be intelligent in several or all of these areas. You are probably extra strong in one or two areas. Look at the following chart to help you understand Dr. Gardner's ideas.

What Dr. Gardner calls it	What the name means	How you learn	Examples of what to include in your portfolio
Visual/Spatial Intelligence	You have visual skills.	You learn by looking at objects and spaces.	A photo of your award-winning science project. A picture of a costume you made for the school play.
Verbal/Linguistic Intelligence	You have language skills.	You learn by reading, writing, speaking, and listening.	An article you wrote that was published in your school newspaper. An award you won for participating in the speech club.
Mathematical/Logical Intelligence	You have math skills.	You learn by working with numbers and by solving problems.	A copy of your SAT math score. A certificate for being in the chess club.
Bodily/Kinesthetic Intelligence	You have physical skills.	You learn by doing things and by using your body.	A letter acknowledging your part in a summer recreation program for children. Your job review following your summer job working for a lawn-care company.

What Dr. Gardner calls it	What the name means	How you learn	Examples of what to include in your portfolio
Musical/Rhythmic Intelligence	You have music and rhythm skills.	You learn by using musical concepts, songs, patterns, and musical instruments.	A letter from your minister describing your participation in the youth choir. A copy of a program showing that your jazz combo played at a wedding reception.
Intrapersonal Intelligence	You have self-awareness skills.	You learn through your natural understanding of your feelings, values, and ideas.	A picture of you with a nursing home resident you read stories to each week. A copy of a neighborhood flyer you prepared to advise neighbors of clean-up day at a nearby park.
Interpersonal Intelligence	You have people skills.	You learn through your natural ability to understand other people. You learn by working in a group or with a partner.	Your grade on a project you and four other students completed in your history class. A program showing that you had a role in your school musical.
Naturalist Intelligence	You have outdoor skills.	You learn from outdoor activities, animals, and field trips. You appreciate the wonder of nature.	A report you wrote following a family trip to a Canadian wildlife preserve. A newspaper article about your involvement with a local hiker's club.
Existential Intelligence	You have mental visualization skills and high ideals.	You learn by looking at the "big picture" of life. You are interested in world issues and in ethical conduct.	An award you won for completing a political survey of your neighborhood. A copy of a letter you sent to a world or religious leader regarding an issue you think is important.

Does this way of organizing your portfolio sound interesting? If so, find more information by searching the Web with the keywords *Multiple Intelligences*.

SCANS Skills

The Secretary's Commission on Achieving Necessary Skills was set up by the U.S. Secretary of Labor. The Commission named several skills that everyone needs in order to succeed. These are referred to as SCANS skills. You can organize your portfolio in sections that show you have the following SCANS skills.

SCANS	What you can do	Examples of what to include in your portfolio
Basic skills	You can read, write, do mathematics, listen, and speak.	A copy of your SAT scores. An article you wrote for your school newspaper.
Thinking skills	You can think creatively, make decisions, solve problems, reason, and learn.	An award you won for participating in the speech club. A picture of a costume you designed for the school play.
Personal qualities	You can be responsible for yourself, maintain self-esteem, be sociable, and have integrity and honesty.	A letter from your minister stating that you are a leader in your youth choir. A picture of you with an elderly person you read to each week.

Tip The third row of the chart above lists important personal qualities. If you don't have these skills, interviewers may not consider you.

Does this way of organizing your portfolio sound interesting? If so, talk to one of your teachers or your school counselor. These adults will be familiar with the SCANS skills and can explain them to you. Also, you can find more information by searching the Web with the keywords *Secretary's Commission Achieving Necessary Skills*.

Self-Exploration

A portfolio organized this way focuses on who you are, what you have done, and what you can do. It includes these sections:

1. Personal Information
2. Values (This section should be short unless you have something especially unusual and significant to include.)
3. Introduction and Personal Reflections (This section also should be short.)
4. Accomplishments and Job History (This section may be short when you first create your portfolio, but it will grow as you get more experience.)
5. Skills and Attributes
6. Education and Training
7. People's Opinions

In addition to these seven sections, you should think about making one other section in your portfolio. Use this as a place where you can file checklists and worksheets from this workbook. Include the ones you decide would be most helpful. You can also include any other materials you choose.

Remember that the information in this extra section will be for your reference only. These are items you want to have handy when you need them.

If you do not want to put this kind of information in your portfolio, you could file it in a separate folder or notebook. Or you may decide to leave the worksheets in the workbook and just keep the book handy for when you need it.

Let's assume you have decided to organize your portfolio around the areas of self-exploration. The following paragraphs describe each section of your portfolio.

PERSONAL INFORMATION. You may think your personal information is just facts about you. But it's more than that. It can actually help you see yourself as other people see you. Having a good idea of who you are helps you in everything you do.

> Locating all these personal documents and getting them all together may be the most time-consuming part of creating your portfolio. It is also one of the most important.

In the Personal Information section of your portfolio, include your

- Birth certificate
- Health records
- Picture identification or current photo
- Social Security card
- Passport
- Driver's license
- Work permit
- Noncitizen status papers
- Survey, test, or assessment results

Include original documents or good photocopies of these items. Then when you need the information, you'll have it.

Locating all these personal documents and getting them all together may be the most time-consuming part of creating your portfolio. It is also one of the most important. You will need this information every time you fill out a school application or interview for a job.

Complete the following worksheet and include it in the Personal Information section of your portfolio. Laws vary from state to state. You may never have to provide all the information listed on the worksheet. However, you should be able to give the information when asked.

About Me

My full name:_____

Street address: _____

City: _____ State/Province: _____ ZIP: _____

Previous address: _____

City: _____ State/Province: _____ ZIP: _____

Contact information: Home:_____ Work: _____

E-mail: _____ Cell phone: _____

Mailing address (if different): _____

City: _____ State/Province: _____ ZIP: _____

Social Security number: _____

Driver's license number: _____

Date of birth: _____ Place of birth: _____

U.S. citizen? (Y/N)_____ If not, current status: _____

Visa: _____ Registration number: _____

VALUES. Your values are the things you think are important. Your values motivate you. If you know what you value, you can decide where you are going and why you want to go there. This can be very helpful when you are selecting a job, a college, or a technical training program.

You may have a hard time thinking of documents to include in the Values section of your portfolio. Your values reflect

- What your family life is like

- What education you have

- Which social groups you belong to

- What you have experienced in life

> Your values are the things you think are important.

Some days you may feel like you're going to be in school forever. But you won't be, of course. Eventually you will finish school and start working. If you find a job that provides you with what you think is important, you will be more content. You will also be a better employee. If you don't find that kind of job, you probably will not be satisfied.

Think about your values when you think about your education, training, and career opportunities. Be sure you make decisions that are in line with your values.

The Values section of your portfolio is closely related to other sections of your portfolio. It should include items that show:

- Your involvement in public and community service activities
- Your leadership roles
- Your involvement in your church
- Your participation in charitable organizations

The activities you are involved in show you and other people what you think is important. In other words, they show what your values are. You will learn more about career and life values in Chapter 3.

One Important Thing

One thing that is important to me is _____

_____

_____

This is one of my values.

INTRODUCTION AND PERSONAL REFLECTIONS. The Introduction and Personal Reflections section is usually at the beginning of a portfolio. However, it may be a section that you write last. It should include a short summary of what you discovered about yourself while putting together your portfolio.

This whole section should be short. It should describe your career and education goals. It is a good place to talk about your major interests and your special abilities.

The information in this section should be autobiographical. For example, you might include a description of a life-changing crisis you faced.

When you show your portfolio to an interviewer, point out the connections between the Introduction and Personal Reflections section and other sections. Emphasize that you are committed to certain educational or career goals. Your explanation will be appreciated by interviewers.

> The Introduction and Personal Reflections section should describe your career and education goals.

My Goals

One education goal I have is _____

_____

One career goal I have is _____

_____

ACCOMPLISHMENTS AND JOB HISTORY. In your Accomplishments and Job History section, include information about any jobs you have had. Describe what you accomplished in those jobs. Include information about both paid and unpaid work experience.

You may not have had a paid job yet, but you probably have had some unpaid work experience. Both are important. Unpaid experience includes volunteer work or service learning. It also includes internships.

> Your portfolio should include information about both paid and unpaid work experience.

You will want to put the following items in this section of your portfolio:

- Your resume (more information in Chapter 8)
- A complete description for each job (paid or unpaid)
- The name and address of each organization
- Your supervisors' names
- Your job evaluations
- References and letters of commendation

Also, if you can, include some things the interviewer can look at, such as artwork, photos, graphs, graphics, and designs. Include any kind of visual information you think would reinforce your message to the interviewer. You will learn more about your accomplishments and job history in Chapter 4.

What I Have Done

One thing I could include in the Accomplishments and Job History section of my portfolio is _____

_____

_____

© JIST Works

SKILLS AND ATTRIBUTES. You may develop skills through formal or informal training. You may also develop skills on the job. Include documents that tell what skills you have that relate to a specific position or to a particular type of schooling. For example, you may have technical, computer, or mechanical skills.

Special knowledge that is needed in one kind of job is also considered a skill. For example, in your classes or at your job, you may have learned how to create a spreadsheet or do a lab experiment.

> If you have skills or knowledge you got from a hobby or something that interests you, include that information in your portfolio.

Also, if you have skills or knowledge you got from a hobby or something that interests you, include that information in your portfolio.

Your attributes are your intangible qualities. They can make the difference between whether you succeed or fail. Some examples of attributes are the ability to

- Communicate well
- Work on team projects
- Learn quickly
- Follow instructions
- Accept criticism
- Be creative

Any information you have that shows that you have these attributes should be part of your portfolio. The Skills and Attributes section of your portfolio gives you the opportunity to really shine. You will learn more about your skills and attributes in Chapter 4.

One Skill

One skill I have is _____

_____

_____

EDUCATION AND TRAINING. In the Education and Training section of your portfolio, include the following:

> Do not just think about your high school experiences. Think about other life experiences you have had.

- High school transcripts
- Course descriptions
- Information about projects you have completed
- Documents that describe seminars and workshops you have completed

Do not just think about your high school experiences. Think about other life experiences you have had. Think about the skills you have learned through nontraditional methods. This kind of learning is called experiential learning.

You will learn more about this section of your portfolio in Chapter 4.

What I Know

One thing I can include in the Education and Training section of my portfolio is _____

_____

_____

PEOPLE'S OPINIONS. If you receive any kind of positive, written statement about your school, work, or community activities, include that in your portfolio. Show interviewers that what people say about you is backed up by the skills and attributes described in your portfolio.

Awards and certificates you've received through volunteer or community service should also be included in this section of your portfolio. If you received an honor from an organization or club, include that. These honors show that you are professional and cooperative. They show you have team spirit. You will learn more about this section of your portfolio in Chapter 4.

> If you receive any kind of positive, written statement about your school, work, or community activities, include that in your portfolio.

What People Say

One item I could include in the People's Opinions section of my portfolio is _____

_____

_____

Getting Your Portfolio Ready

 Tip   Your portfolio won't help you much if it looks or feels sloppy.

You should now have a general idea about the kinds of things to include in your portfolio. But how do you take those things and present them to an interviewer? Your portfolio won't help you much if it looks or feels sloppy.

The following information refers to paper-based portfolios:

- Use original documents wherever you can. You can also use clean, clear photo-copies if you don't want to risk ruining the documents.

- Put each document in a transparent plastic cover (a sheet protector).

- Use separators and labels to divide the sections of your portfolio. Type the labels.

- Use a three-ring binder. If you have artwork or other large materials, you might need to use an artist-type portfolio case.

- Be sure the binder is not too large or too small for the number of documents you include.

- Include a cover sheet on the front of the binder. Use a computer to create clever and original graphic designs. Indicate that this is a portfolio. Give your name, address, e-mail address, and telephone number. Stay away from designs that are too wild.

- During an interview, you may want to just put the items in a briefcase so you can pull them out as you need them.

- Graphs, pictures, drawings, blueprints, designs, and any other visual aids should look appealing and should be in color, if possible.

- Handle your portfolio carefully. Clean off any smudges or handprints.

The way your portfolio looks can make a big difference in your interview. The way you present your material can give you an advantage.

Portfolio Supplies

The check marks below show the items I will need for putting together my portfolio.

_____ Copies of documents that will be included

_____ Several sheet protectors

_____ Pages for separating the sections

_____ Labels

_____ A three-ring binder

_____ A cover sheet

_____ A briefcase

_____ Other: _____

_____ Other: _____

Portfolios and Interviews

When you think about interviews, you may wonder how many interviews you will have. The answer is that during your life you will have many interviews. You may interview for admission to colleges or technical schools. You may interview for jobs, for internships, or for leadership positions in community agencies.

Remember that a quick review of your portfolio will not tell the interviewer what you can do. You should be prepared to describe each item.

Before the Interview

Be ready to talk about your portfolio examples as you show them to an interviewer. This requires three things:

> **B**e ready to talk about your portfolio examples as you show them to an interviewer.

preparation, preparation, and preparation

Identify items in your portfolio that relate to the interview. Think about how you can describe each of those items to the interviewer. You can think of these descriptions as short stories. Practice saying each "story" aloud. Make sure no "story" is longer than 1 1/2 minutes.

In your "story," you might

- Describe one of your skills or accomplishments
- Describe a problem or need you faced
- Describe the action you took to solve a problem or meet a need
- Describe the results

Remember that you want to convince the interviewer to choose you. Being modest at an interview is not a virtue. You will learn more about interviews in Chapter 8.

Look back at the worksheet called "What I Know" on page 18. Then write a "story" about the item you named.

A Short Story

Here's a "story" about the item I described in the worksheet "What I Know."

_____

_____

_____

_____

During the Interview

When you interview for admission to a school or training program, choose items in your portfolio that relate to what you want to study. When you interview for a job, choose items that relate to the position you want. Describe what you do well.

> Interviewers want to help candidates they think are qualified.

Interviewers want to help candidates they think are qualified. Describe and show examples of what you have done and what you can do.

By the end of the interview, you may know you are interested in the job or school. If so, express your interest to the interviewer. Describe why you want the job or why you want to attend a certain school. Then ask the interviewer if he or she has any concerns about your ability to do the job or to be successful in the school. Think about what the interviewer says. Answer the interviewer's questions.

WHAT'S NEXT?

This chapter gave you a general understanding of portfolios. You thought about what a portfolio is and how you can use one. You considered options for organizing your portfolio.

In Chapter 2, you will learn the specifics of putting your portfolio together. And you will get ideas about creating an electronic portfolio.

Chapter 2

More About Portfolios

Chapter 1 introduced you to portfolios. You are now ready for some specifics. This chapter will help you answer these questions:

- What steps should I follow in creating my portfolio?

- What is an electronic portfolio? Do I need one?

- How do I create a Web site?

- What are some things I should or should not do when preparing my portfolio?

Finding a job is hard work. Getting additional training or education after high school is hard work. If you're prepared and organized, you'll have a better chance of succeeding. You can use your portfolio to show admissions officers and employers who you are and who you can be.

What to Do

In Chapter 1, we noted that there is no standard way of organizing a portfolio. What is important is to organize your portfolio in a way that seems logical to you. Start with a set of goals and objectives. Keep in mind that interviewers are looking for people who have the skills and attributes they need.

> Your portfolio is a marketing tool. And **you** are what is being marketed.

Your portfolio is a marketing tool. And **you** are what is being marketed. You must

- Understand your strengths and weaknesses
- Set meaningful goals
- Seek out courses, activities, jobs, internships, and other opportunities that fit your skills and interests

Creating and developing your portfolio isn't easy. And that's just the beginning. You should update your portfolio often. And remember that the more school and work experience you get, the more interviewers will expect from you. You must show them that you can do what they expect. Your portfolio can help you do that.

Creating a portfolio is rewarding. It means that you have to look at where you have been, where you are now, and where you want to be. It can help you take control of your education and career.

You will keep learning and developing for a lifetime. You must make decisions that will help you reach your goals. The portfolio is a tool that can help make this possible.

Get Started

Before you start putting your portfolio together, take a look at who you are. Think about what you can do, what you can do well, and what your goals are. Think about the following questions. Make lists of your responses.

> Before you start putting your portfolio together, take a look at who you are. Think about what you can do, what you can do well, and what your goals are.

- **Who am I?** What have I accomplished? What can I do? What do I do well? What would I like to do better? What do I know? What am I interested in?

- **What opportunities do I have?** What characteristics do I have that match what interviewers are looking for? What kinds of schools and organizations am I interested in?

- **What are my goals?** What school or career interests me the most?

- **How can I present myself to interviewers?** How can I be sure they understand my main message? What can I do to create a good first impression?

This may be the first time you have thought about who you are. Be thorough. Start collecting items to include in your portfolio. A logical pattern will begin to emerge. If you follow this pattern, you can create a portfolio that truly reflects who you are. This portfolio will allow you to move ahead in your education and career.

Are you planning to go through a training program after high school to learn how to do a certain job? If so, you will be interested to know that many careers are represented by organizations that

- Set standards for their members

- Describe what people in that career should be able to do

- Tell how these people should conduct their business

- Help members set goals for improving their skills

- Help members set a realistic time frame for reaching their goals

Look for organizations for people in careers that interest you. Ask them for information. This will help you understand what will be expected of you. It will help you realize what skills you need to develop and what courses you need to take. If you join one of these organizations, include that information in your portfolio. For more information, check out the Web site at http://info.asaenet.org/gateway/onlineassocslist.html.

I Define Myself

Here's a description of who I am.

_____

_____

Think About What to Include

 You have to know who you are and what you want before you can decide what items to put in your portfolio.

In Chapter 1, you examined several categories of material you should collect. Now you have to choose what is the best material in each category. Your decision will be based on the goals you set. Here are two examples:

- Your goal might be to find a position involving leadership. If so, put items in your portfolio that show that you have been and are a leader. This can include things that are not work related, such as coaching a children's soccer team.

- Your goal might be to pursue a technical career. If so, put things in your portfolio that prove that you have technical skills, such as working on cars.

These are just two examples. You can probably think of lots more. The point is that you have to know who you are and what you want before you can decide what items to put in your portfolio.

Look at the following worksheet. The examples on the worksheet may not match your interests. But they will show you how to match goals to items you can include in your portfolio. Mark each item true or false and then briefly explain your answer.

Content

My goal is to work with children. In the Values section of my portfolio, I should include the thank-you note I received from the principal after I tutored two younger students.
T_____ F_____

Explanation: _____

_____

_____

I am interested in a career in auto mechanics. In the Skills and Attributes section of my portfolio, I would probably <u>not</u> need to include the thank-you note from my principal.
T_____ F_____

Explanation: _____

_____

_____

I want to enroll in a training program for paralegals. In the Education and Training section of my portfolio, I would want to include a copy of my Honors Roll certificates.
T_____ F_____

Explanation: _____

_____

_____

Decide How to Organize Your Portfolio

Now you are ready to build your portfolio. Again, you can arrange the various sections in any order. Organize your portfolio in a way that will help you reach your goals. Remember that you want to use your portfolio to get a job or to get accepted into a college or training program.

> Remember that you want to use your portfolio to get a job or to get accepted into a college or training program.

No matter how you organize your portfolio, you should begin with a simple table of contents. Refer to Chapter 1 to review three suggested ways of organizing your portfolio.

Chapter 1, pages 9–13, describes three ways to organize your portfolio. It's time now to think about which method of organization you will use. Complete the following worksheet.

25

I Decide

The type of portfolio organization I think would be best for me is

_____ Multiple Intelligences

_____ SCANS Skills

_____ Self-Exploration

Here's why. _____

_____

_____

Look at the Results

There are no set rules for judging your final portfolio. Here are some suggestions:

- **Review your portfolio yourself.** This gives you an opportunity to think about whether your plans for your education and career are really right for you. You may decide you should choose another path and head in a different direction. If you like where you're going, your portfolio can help you get there.

- **Ask someone else to look at your portfolio.** Ask them if they think the portfolio reflects your goals.

- **Use your portfolio in an interview.** After the interview, decide if your portfolio was effective. Make changes if you need to.

Portfolio Review

Here's the name of someone I can ask to review my portfolio.

_____

This person would be a good person to ask because _____

_____

_____

Electronic Portfolios

The question of whether to go electronic is fast becoming a no-brainer. Soon, people will probably not be considered for employment or for school admission if they do not have documents that can be transmitted electronically. This is especially true for people in creative careers. But it is also true for anyone who uses technology in his or her work.

Almost all students and employees are expected to be able to use a computer. You will at least want to have an electronic version of your resume that can be e-mailed to interviewers. You may also want to scan other portfolio documents to create electronic files that can be e-mailed. Proofread the scanned documents carefully for scanning errors.

Be Careful

Electronic media are all the rage. Personal Web sites and portfolios on CD (compact disc) are common. Things you take for granted weren't even available to your parents. You might assume that these electronic formats will replace hardcopy versions of the portfolio. But that's not the case. Why?

- People do not have time to consider everything you might include on a CD or Web site. They don't even have time to look at all the resumes they receive. When you have an interview, you can focus on specific parts of the portfolio.

- People may just see your CD or Web site as presenting a group of unrelated documents. However, when you talk to an interviewer in person, you can describe how the items are related.

- People who just look at your CD or Web site do not get to know you personally. When you have an interview, you and the interviewer meet each other face to face. You get to know each other at least a little. You can both decide whether you are a good match.

Uses for an Electronic Portfolio

You should always have a hardcopy portfolio. But you should also think about having an electronic portfolio. Why?

- An electronic portfolio is not expensive to create.

- An electronic portfolio lets you update your information easily.

- An electronic portfolio can reach a lot of people in a short time.

> An electronic portfolio will not get you a job, but it might get you an interview.

- An electronic portfolio gets your information to people who would not otherwise know who you are.

Interviewers will probably just take a quick look at your CD or Web site. Still, you can use these tools to create a positive impression. Electronic portfolios are still relatively new. Interviewers might stop to look at your portfolio if it catches their eye. An electronic portfolio will not get you a job, but it might get you an interview.

Usually, what you put in your electronic portfolio will be the same as what you put in your paper version. However, there's one important point to remember. When you are meeting with an interviewer, you can decide which items to show the person. When an interviewer is looking at your CD or Web site, they decide for themselves what to look at. This means you must be careful what you include. One thing you should always include is a text version of your resume.

An electronic portfolio is an exciting tool. Don't overlook it. Use your technical abilities and be creative. Even a beginner can learn to create electronic documents fairly quickly.

You can use software programs such as Microsoft PowerPoint to make your documents more interesting. Graphics software such as Adobe Photoshop can add color, design, emphasis, and special effects.

Creating CDs and Web Sites

If you put your portfolio on CD, you can easily mail or give a copy to an interviewer. But remember, you will not be able to change the CD after you give it to someone. You can change your Web site, however.

> You can find many Web sites that will help you create your electronic portfolio.

You could hire someone to create your Web site, but you would probably have to pay about $1,000. That's probably not a good option, right?

If you do not want to pay someone else, try designing a Web site on your own. It's not hard, and it doesn't cost much. Look for some inexpensive, easy-to-use software. To create your own Web site, you need three things:

1. **Web-creation software.** You can buy software for as little as $50. Or maybe you can use your school computer lab. Web-creation software shows you how to create a Web site. It tells you how to register with a Web hosting service and shows you how to get started. For information about software, search the Web with the keywords *Web Site Software*.

2. **A domain name or URL (Uniform Resource Locator).** Technically, the terms *domain name* and *URL* have different definitions, but they are often used interchangeably. Your domain name is your Web address.

    You can make up any name or combination of names to use as your domain name. Check online for availability. Register the name with one of the online domain name services. Current costs are about $50 for three years. You have to renew the name or you can lose it. The services will remind you when it is time to renew. For information about registering a domain name, simply search the Web with the keywords *Domain Name*. You will find sources and instructions for registering.

3. **A Web hosting service.** This is the organization that maintains your Web site. One thing the service does is create an e-mail mailbox for you. Ask about the cost of the service. For about $10 per month, you get basic service but very little help. For about $25 per month, you can get some real help. You can get information about these services by searching the Web with the keywords *Web Hosting Services*.

You can find many Web sites that will help you create your electronic portfolio. Following is a partial list of what is available:

www.rit.edu (Keyword: Portfolio)

amby.com/kimeldorf

www.ash.udel.edu

transition.Alaska.edu/www/portfolios.html

electronicportfolios.com

www.quintcareers.com/career_portfolios.html

www.wa.gov/esd/lmea/soicc/prtfolio.htm

www.datasync.com/~teachers/portfolio.html

www.bsu.edu/students/careers/documents/portfoli/

bcrc.bio.umass.edu/presentations/portfolios_ppt.pdf

My Web Site

One word that describes how I feel about creating a Web site is _____

One reason why I might not create a Web site is _____

_____

_____

_____

Things to Remember

☑ Give people your Web address. List it on your resume and letters. Whenever you tell someone your telephone number, give them your Web address, too.

☑ Limit how much information you put on your Web site. The important thing is content. Carefully choose what to include. Be sure it looks professional.

☑ Update your Web site frequently. Your hosting service can help you with this.

☑ Avoid using fancy, space-eating graphics. You want interviewers to be able to download your Web site quickly.

☑ Tell interviewers how to contact you by telephone, fax, and e-mail.

☑ Look at other Web sites. Ask your friends for suggestions. Ask your parents or other adults, too. Have at least one person look at your Web site before you "go live."

☑ Make color copies of the information on your Web site. Refer to Chapter 1 for suggestions on how to use your portfolio in an interview.

☑ Keep your Web site simple and honest. Be sure none of the information or graphics are offensive.

☑ Target your electronic portfolio to a certain audience. Choose people or companies that match your education and career goals. The term *spam* refers to unsolicited e-mail. Avoid using spam.

☑ Leave out blinking lights, pop-up screens, fancy fonts, or other gimmicks.

☑ Include just a little personal information on your Web site. Don't include your picture. You want to get interviews, but you also want to be safe. Anyone who has access to the Internet can look at your Web site.

> You already have tools on your computer that let you know how much room your graphics take up. Put your cursor on the graphic image. Right-click the mouse. Look at the screen that pops up. Click the line that says "properties." It will tell you how many bytes your graphic takes up. Your Web hosting service can help you be sure your graphics show up like you want them to without using up too many bytes.

The Internet Is Important

On page 4 in Chapter 1, you read a short definition of the term *self-direction*. In today's world, you must be prepared and flexible. You have to keep learning—no matter how old you are. Also, you have to be able to communicate with interviewers. You have to tell them what you can do and what you know. You have to show them that you have potential.

> The world changes quickly. This can make you feel helpless. But the Internet connects all of us in new and exciting ways.

So how can you cope? Colleges and training programs change their admission requirements. Jobs come and go. Companies start up and then fold. Decisions in faraway places influence your life. Using the Internet can help you cope with these changes. The Internet provides information that was not available before. It helps you look for opportunities in other parts of the world. It lets you communicate with interviewers everywhere.

The world changes quickly. This can make you feel helpless. But the Internet connects all of us in new and exciting ways. It opens doors and reveals some amazing opportunities. You can use the Internet to respond to change.

WHAT'S NEXT?

This chapter showed you how to start putting your student portfolio together. It gave you some information about how you can create a Web site.

The information in Chapter 3 will move you closer to a good understanding of yourself. It will help you think about who you are.

Part Two

Understanding Yourself

Chapter 3

Who You Are

Y ou have interests, abilities, and values that make you unique. As you create your portfolio, you will need to understand who you are. This will help you get the education you need and find a satisfying career. In this chapter, you will find answers to these questions:

- What is important to me in my life, education, and career?

- How do I learn best?

- What words describe my personality?

- What self-management skills do I have? Can I make decisions? Am I willing to take risks? Do I know how to manage my time and deal with stress? Do I know what to do to stay physically and emotionally healthy?

- What are my past, current, and future roles in life? How do these roles affect my education and career decisions?

- What kind of education and work am I most interested in?

You may want to include the worksheets in this chapter in your portfolio. You can include them wherever you think they fit best. Think about how you are organizing your portfolio. Refer to Chapter 1 to review the three types of organization described there.

Most of these worksheets are not intended to be shown to interviewers. But they can serve as valuable references for you. They will help you build and organize your portfolio and consider education and career options.

Values

People can often tell what you value by looking at who you are. Your values motivate you at school, at home, and at work. You have certain ideas about what is important. If you can balance what is important in each area of your life, you have a better chance of finding satisfaction.

> People can often tell what you value by looking at who you are.

Explore various education and career options. As you look at each option, think about what is important to you. You will not find many education and career options that match all of your values. However, the options you choose should fulfill many of your important values. After you talk to an interviewer, compare your list of values to what the educational or career option offers you.

Career Values

Even though you are still in high school, you should be thinking about what kind of work you want to do in future. Also, if you plan to get a part-time job as a student, this information can help you decide what you want to do.

> If you value the work you do, you are more committed to working and to doing the job.

If you value the work you do, you are more committed to working and to doing the job. Here are a few examples of work values:

- Income level
- Safety
- Work environment
- Skills development
- Teamwork
- Change and variety
- Independence
- Creativity
- Competition
- Advancement
- Structure and security
- Physical challenges
- Helping others
- Taking risks

If you have a hard time identifying what you value, talk with your friends and family. They may see things you do not see. Self-assessment "tests" can also help you discover more about your values. At least one of these is probably available free at your school.

The following worksheet will help you think about your career values. Use check marks to show how important each career value is to you. Some things will only be important to you now as a student worker. Some things will only be important to you later, when you look for work after you finish school. Many things will be important to you in both situations.

My Career Values

Now	Later		Very Important	Somewhat Important	Not At All Important
____	____	Being successful	_____	_____	_____
____	____	Being important	_____	_____	_____
____	____	Having power	_____	_____	_____
____	____	Being in charge	_____	_____	_____
____	____	Fitting in	_____	_____	_____
____	____	Knowing what to do	_____	_____	_____
____	____	Doing something hard	_____	_____	_____
____	____	Being able to compete	_____	_____	_____
____	____	Helping others	_____	_____	_____
____	____	Influencing others	_____	_____	_____
____	____	Working alone	_____	_____	_____
____	____	Using my creativity	_____	_____	_____
____	____	Feeling good about myself	_____	_____	_____
____	____	Making money	_____	_____	_____
____	____	Having a set routine	_____	_____	_____
____	____	Having a changeable routine	_____	_____	_____
____	____	Feeling peaceful	_____	_____	_____
____	____	Having a good reputation	_____	_____	_____
____	____	Being respected	_____	_____	_____
____	____	Being responsible	_____	_____	_____
____	____	Being secure	_____	_____	_____

Life Values

Tip Be sure your list of values reflects what **you** think is important, not what **others** say should be important.

You've thought about what is and will be important to you in your job or career. Now think about those things that are important to you outside of work. This would include your years as a high school student. Here are a few examples of life values:

- Leisure time
- Family
- Hobbies or sports
- Friendships
- Community activities
- Religious activities

One way to understand your values is to think about unpleasant experiences. For example, maybe your younger brother does not do well in science class this semester. You and your brother both want him to do better in school. You realize that finding time to help your brother is important to you.

You can also think about your life values by recalling happy experiences.

On the following worksheet, create a list of ten life values that are important to you. Then number the values in order of their importance to you. Share the list with people who know you well. Ask them if it matches what they know about you. Be sure your list of values reflects what **you** think is important, not what **others** say should be important.

My Life Values

Here's a list of the ten life values that are most important to me. I've numbered them to show the order of their importance.

_____   _____

_____   _____

_____   _____

_____   _____

_____   _____

_____   _____

_____   _____

_____   _____

_____   _____

_____   _____

Learning Styles

What does the term *learning style* mean? It means *the way you learn*. In Chapter 4 of this book, you will think about the skills you have now and the skills you want to develop. When you are trying to learn new skills, you need to know what your learning style is.

Remember that learning does not just take place at school. You can see an example of this in your own life: You are a student for only a few years. You are a learner for a lifetime.

> When you are trying to learn new skills, you need to know what your learning style is.

Does everybody learn the same way? No. Here is a short description of two types of learning:

1. **Traditional learning.** This kind of learning is also called *classroom learning*. Some people learn best by reading books and listening to lectures. They learn by taking part in activities that are led by a teacher.

2. **Experiential learning.** Some people prefer to learn by doing something. They like to practice or experiment.

Think about which of these two categories describes you. You will probably find that both ways apply to you. But you will also find that one way is best. If you know what kind of learner you are, you will have a better chance of being successful. This information helps you take responsibility for your learning.

One of your teachers or your school counselor will probably have a survey you can take to find out what kind of learner you are. One example is the *Kolb Learning Style Inventory* (LSI). If you use a survey like the LSI, include the results in your portfolio.

After you know what kind of learner you are, you may want to make some changes. For example, you might find that you are basically a traditional learner. You like to learn by reading books. If so, try learning something by just doing it. Try learning something without reading a book or watching a video about it. This will help you become more of an experiential learner.

Interviewers prefer people who can learn in the traditional way and through experience. Use your portfolio to show interviewers that you are that kind of person.

The following worksheet will help you think about how you learn best.

My Learning Style

When I need to learn something new, I learn best by

_____ Reading about it

_____ Seeing it

_____ Seeing someone do it

_____ Listening to someone explain it

_____ Doing it myself

_____ Working with a small group to figure it out

I have looked at the descriptions of traditional learning and experiential learning.

_____ I am mostly a traditional learner.

_____ I am mostly an experiential learner.

Personality Styles

Learning new skills is easier if you know what your learning style is. Learning is also easier if you know something about your personality. Your personality affects your decisions about

- Whether to get more training or education after high school
- Where you want to go to school
- What you choose to do as a career

The following chart gives examples of how your personality affects what career you choose.

If you like to...	Do not select a career in which...
Have lots of change and variety	You do the same thing every day
Meet and talk to new people	You work alone in an office
Plan your activities	You have constant interruptions

Ask your teacher or school counselor about personality tests. These adults will have a survey you can take to learn more about your personality. If you take a personality survey, include the results in your portfolio.

> As you mature and grow, your personality changes.

As you mature and grow, your personality changes. Use the following worksheet to think about your personality style.

My Personality Style

Two ways to describe my behavior at school are

1. _____

2. _____

Two ways to describe my behavior at home are

1. _____

2. _____

continues

continued

Two ways I react to new situations are

1. _____

2. _____

I would describe my personality as

_____

_____

People say my personality is

_____

_____

Self-Management Styles

Self-management is a big word. *Self-management style* describes the way you handle life. It refers to

- Making decisions
- Taking risks
- Managing your time
- Dealing with stress
- Staying healthy
- Finding emotional support

If you know how to manage your life as a student, you will have an easier time managing your career.

Maybe you do not always like the way you handle things in your life. If so, you're not alone. The good news is that self-management skills can be learned. Talk to people you admire. Ask them about how they manage their lives. Visit a bookstore or library for more information.

If you know how to manage your life as a student, you will have an easier time managing your career. The worksheets on the following pages will show you whether your self-management style works for you.

Making Decisions

How do you usually make decisions? Look at the following chart. The examples involve a fairly easy decision. But the process is the same for any education or career decision.

You may want to add this chart to your portfolio. Refer to it when you are considering career and life changes.

Define the problem. State the goal. List alternative solutions. Collect information. Compare several alternatives. Choose one alternative. Take action on your choice. Review your choice. Make new decisions.

What to do	Example
Define the problem. Do not just look at the surface problem. See if you can decide what the underlying problem is. Be specific. State the problem as a question.	Can I go to the movie with my friends tonight and still finish my math assignment?
State the goal. Clearly describe how you want things to turn out.	I do not want to bring my math score down by not finishing my homework. I also want to go to the movie with my friends.
List ways to solve the problem. Think about which things are safe and which require risk. Think about what might be the outcome of each solution.	I could tell my friends I do not have time for a movie tonight. That would be a safe decision. I would be sure to get my assignment done. Or I could take a risk and go to the movie. Then I would have to stay up late, and I might not finish my assignment.
Collect information. Describe the kind of information you need and where you can get it. Decide if the information is relevant to the problem.	I need to call one of my friends to find out what time the movie begins and ends. I need to ask my friends if they could go to the movie another night. I need to figure out how long it will take me to finish my assignment.
Compare your choices. See which choices match what you think is important. Think about which ones allow you to keep the commitments you have made to other people. Describe what people or things are available to help you with each choice. Think about what restrictions you have.	Going to the movie lets me spend time with my friends. Doing my homework will help me get into the college I have picked out. I will talk to my parents about what they think I should do.
Choose one alternative. Decide which choice matches your goals best.	I will stay home tonight. I want to be sure to do well in math. I can spend time with my friends another night.
Take action on your choice. Decide what you will do now that you have made a choice. Decide what actions you can take now and later.	I will call one of my friends to let everyone know that I am not going to the movie. I will start my homework assignment now so I will not have to stay up too late.
Review your choice. Do this often, especially as your situation changes.	Last week I decided not to go to the movie because I had a huge math assignment to finish. This week I might be able to go. I do not have as much homework.
Make new decisions. A choice that is good for you today may not be good for you next year.	Now that I am a senior, I need to spend time visiting colleges. I am going to spend less time going to movies.

Taking Risks

All decisions involve some level of risk. Your decisions are influenced by how much risk you are willing to take. The following information helps you understand risks.

> All decisions involve some level of risk. Your decisions are influenced by how much risk you are willing to take.

Decision	Risk	Example
I've decided to accept a job as an office clerk in a law firm.	I might make a decision I won't be happy with later.	Working as an office clerk doesn't let me have enough contact with other people.
I've decided to attend Ohio State University in the fall.	I might not be able to follow through with what I decide to do.	I don't want to stay at Ohio State. It's too far from my home.
I've decided to accept an internship with a local computer software company.	I might miss an opportunity to do something else.	Because of my internship, I won't be able to take a full class load at school this semester.

When thinking about the risks involved in your decisions, you might

- Consider several options and then choose the one that's most likely to be successful
- Give up what you want, just to avoid risk
- Choose the first thing that comes to your mind
- Let someone else make your decisions for you
- Just do what you feel is right
- Postpone taking any action
- Give up and let whatever happens, happen
- Become overwhelmed by the risks and options
- Think carefully about your decision and choose something you feel good about
- Take whatever risks are necessary to be sure you reach your desired outcome

Which of these do you think are good responses?

During your life you will have to make many decisions. You will make decisions about looking for a job, changing jobs, or getting more education or training. These decisions may seem exciting to you. Or they may feel risky. Making these decisions may even make you feel upset.

Think about these questions:

- Do some things seem risky just because I don't know much about them?
- Who do I know who has faced the same risks I face?
- What might happen if I take this risk?
- What might happen if I don't take the risk?
- What can I do to make my decision less risky?

The following worksheet can help you understand your risk-taking style more clearly.

My Risk-Taking Style

Sometimes I am faced with several changes at once. One important decision I made was

_____

I was comfortable with the change.   Yes____   No____

Making the decision was easy.   Yes____   No____

As a student, I have taken the following risks:

_____

_____

_____

Good things that have happened because I took a risk:

_____

_____

_____

Managing Time

Are you going to be exploring careers? Choosing a college or training program? Looking for work? If so, you will need a lot of time and energy. And you are probably already very busy. If you want to do well in school or on the job, you have to manage your time.

> If you want to do well in school or on the job, you have to manage your time.

Here are some questions to ask yourself:

- Am I satisfied with how I manage my time? Think about the time you spend working on school projects and assignments. Think about the time you spend at work and after work. Think about the time you spend on other activities.

- Can I improve my time-management skills?

- Do I spend enough time doing what is most important to me?

- What keeps me from doing what is important to me?

If you are not satisfied with how you manage your time, talk to your teachers and school counselors. Ask these adults to suggest books or tapes that might help you.

Use the following worksheet to start evaluating and understanding your time-management style.

My Time-Management Style

When I have a lot of things to do, I manage my time by

_____

_____

_____

When faced with school or work deadlines, I usually

_____

_____

_____

Dealing with Stress

Tip   Often, a situation appears hopeless until you step back and reevaluate it.

Your health makes a big impact on what you do with your life. Some health problems are out of your control, of course. But many are not.

Have you ever heard someone say, "I'm really stressed out"? They probably mean they've got too much to do. Or they may mean they are facing a difficult situation.

Another word for *stress* is *tension*. Sometimes you are torn between two or more things you want to do or have to do. That causes tension. That is stress.

Stress can be caused by

- The death of someone you love
- Your parents' divorce
- Changing schools
- Not having the money to do what you need or want to do

If you are under stress for a long time, your body will be affected. This makes you less able to prevent illness.

Whether you are in school or working, you will face many changes. These changes can cause stress. Every situation has advantages and disadvantages. When you are in a stressful situation, consider the following questions:

- What are the advantages and disadvantages of my situation?
- Is there something I can do to change my situation?
- What might happen if I do nothing?
- Is my attitude toward the situation likely to change?
- Does this situation affect my long-term career and life plans?

Often, a situation appears hopeless until you step back and reevaluate it. Talk with people whose opinions you value and trust. Many resources are available to help you identify and deal with stress.

The following worksheet will help you see how vulnerable you are to stress. Evaluate yourself on each of the items listed below. Use the numbers shown at the top of the worksheet. Page 45 tells you how to score your answers.

How I Deal with Stress

1 = strongly disagree   **4** = slightly agree

2 = disagree   **5** = agree

3 = slightly disagree   **6** = strongly agree

	1	2	3	4	5	6
I eat at least two balanced meals a day.	1	2	3	4	5	6
I get 7 to 8 hours of sleep each night.	1	2	3	4	5	6
I give and receive affection regularly.	1	2	3	4	5	6
I am close to my family. We rely on each other.	1	2	3	4	5	6
I exercise to the point of perspiration at least three times per week.	1	2	3	4	5	6
I do not smoke.	1	2	3	4	5	6
I am the appropriate weight for my height.	1	2	3	4	5	6
My basic physical needs are taken care of.	1	2	3	4	5	6
I get strength from my religious beliefs.	1	2	3	4	5	6
I regularly attend club or social activities.	1	2	3	4	5	6
I do not drink or use drugs.	1	2	3	4	5	6
I have a lot of friends and I know a lot of people.	1	2	3	4	5	6
I have several close friends I can talk to about personal things.	1	2	3	4	5	6
I am in good health, including my eyes, ears, and teeth.	1	2	3	4	5	6
I am able to speak openly about my feelings when I'm angry or worried.	1	2	3	4	5	6
I have regular conversations with family members about problems, chores, money, and other daily-living issues.	1	2	3	4	5	6
I do something for fun at least once per week.	1	2	3	4	5	6
I am able to organize my time effectively.	1	2	3	4	5	6
I drink less than three cups of tea or cola per day.	1	2	3	4	5	6
I take quiet time for myself during the day.	1	2	3	4	5	6

Total Stress-Vulnerability Score = _____

If you have a score of **70 or more**, you can probably handle stress well. However, if you are facing several changes in your life, you may be more stressed than you usually are. Take care of yourself.

If you have a score from **41 through 69**, you can probably handle stress. But you need to have a stress-management plan. Design a plan and stick with it.

If you have a score of **40 or less**, you probably cannot handle stress well. Review the quiz you just completed. List the items that received the lowest scores. Make some changes to bring those scores up. Take your physical and emotional health seriously.

Staying Physically Healthy

When your body is healthy, you can handle stress better. Two ways to stay healthy are to eat a balanced diet and to exercise regularly. You probably already know that exercise and a good diet can make you look better. They can also help relieve stress and prevent illness.

> You know you will have times when you feel stressed. Decide now that you will not do things to make your situation worse. Don't add to your problems.

Before starting any special diet or exercise program, check with your doctor, school nurse, or physical education teacher. These adults can give you some valuable advice.

You know you will have times when you feel stressed. Decide now that you will not do things to make your situation worse. Don't add to your problems. Consider making these promises to yourself:

- I won't abuse alcohol or other drugs.
- I won't stop eating, but I won't overeat.
- I won't make a habit of staying in bed all day.
- I won't lose control of my temper or become violent.

You can find many agencies, people, or programs to help you. Check out the listings in your telephone book or ask an adult you trust.

Eat a Balanced Diet

Machinery cannot operate without fuel. And your body cannot function well unless you provide it with a healthy, balanced diet. If you want help with eating well, the following people can provide guidance:

- Your doctor
- Your parents
- Your school counselor
- Your health teacher and other teachers

> Your body cannot function well unless you provide it with a healthy, balanced diet.

Watch out for foods that have too much or too little fat, fiber, salt, iron, vitamins, caffeine, and cholesterol. Think about the benefits and dangers of what you eat. Use what you have learned in school. Use your common sense. Keep yourself energized.

Exercise Regularly

When you are under stress, your body produces extra adrenaline. Exercising uses up this excess adrenaline and produces helpful chemicals. These chemicals are called endorphins. They ease tension and improve your mood. They give you a sense of well-being.

> Regular exercise helps your body ward off many illnesses, including ones caused by stress.

Regular exercise helps your body ward off many illnesses, including ones caused by stress. If you are physically healthy, you will also be more mentally healthy. Check with your doctor, parents, teachers, and counselors to decide what kind of exercise is best for you.

The worksheet titled "How I Deal with Stress" (page 44) includes several items about keeping your body healthy. The following worksheet will help you think specifically about your strategy for staying physically healthy.

My Physical Health

I would describe my current physical health as _____

_____

_____

I have these concerns about my physical health: _____

_____

_____

One thing I could do to improve my eating habits is _____

_____

_____

One thing I could do to improve my exercise habits is _____

_____

_____

Finding Emotional Support

 Tip Difficult times in your life are easier to handle if you don't try to handle them alone.

The previous section of this chapter is called "Staying Physically Healthy." It explains that your physical health affects your ability to deal with stress. The same is true of your emotional health.

Difficult times in your life are easier to handle if you don't try to handle them alone. You need an emotional support system.

Some people describe change as like being on an emotional roller coaster. When you face change or stress, you may feel

- Relief
- Anger
- Hope
- Excitement

- Sadness
- Depression
- Disappointment
- Happiness

Regardless of the situation, most students welcome the opportunity to talk about what they are going through. Talking makes you feel better and think more clearly. It helps you decide what to do. For emotional support, talk to people who

- Will listen to your feelings
- Can care about you without getting involved in your situation
- Know how to give encouragement
- Have a positive attitude
- Believe in you and know what you can do

You'll find that no one person is able to give you all the support you need in every situation. Try to meet people who have had experiences similar to yours. Locate people who are trained to give emotional support and encouragement.

Also, remember that you should be supportive of the people who give you support.

The worksheet titled "How I Deal with Stress" (page 44) includes several items about finding emotional support. The following worksheet will help you think specifically about your emotional health. Include the completed worksheet in your portfolio.

My Emotional Health

I would describe my current emotional health as _____

_____

_____

I have these concerns about my emotional health:_____

_____

_____

When I need to make a decision, I talk to_____

_____

_____

One way I could get more emotional support is _____

_____

_____

Life Roles

Life roles refers to the way you function in a certain situation. It tells what your part is in the overall picture. For example, during your life, you will probably be a child, a student, an employee, a parent, and a partner. In each role you develop new skills and discover new opportunities. Each role helps you decide what is important.

> *Life roles* refers to the way you function in a certain situation. It tells what your part is in the overall picture.

Many things work together to determine what your roles will be. When you are deciding how to spend your time and energy, think about your life roles. Ask yourself the following questions:

- What is important to me? To my family? To my background and culture?
- Has my gender affected my role in life?
- Has my cultural or ethnic background determined what I am expected to do?
- What rules did my family have about who should do what?
- What current family circumstances affect my roles?
- Do my past and current relationships affect my roles?

Changing Life Roles

Life roles change. Sometimes you will focus on only one role. At other times, you will balance several roles. As you plan your education and career, think about your past, current, and future roles.

The following worksheet will help you think about how your roles change. In the first part of the worksheet, check the roles you have now. Skip the roles that do not apply to you. Write a brief description of each role you check.

In the last part of the worksheet, list your past roles and probable future roles. The first part of the worksheet can give you some possibilities.

My Changing Life Roles

The check marks below indicate life roles I have **now.** I've briefly described each of these roles.

_____ Student_____

_____ Athlete _____

_____ Volunteer_____

_____ Friend _____

_____ Driver _____

_____ Child _____

_____ Brother/sister _____

_____ Employee_____

_____ Job seeker _____

_____ Other _____

Three roles I've had **in the past:**

_____

_____

_____

Three roles I expect to have **in the future:**

_____

_____

_____

Balancing Life Roles

Think about how you balance the roles you have now. For example, if you are planning to get a part-time job, you will have to make room in your life for that new role. Instead of just being a student, you will be a student and an employee. Think about how much time and energy each of your current roles takes. Think about which of your life roles is most important to you.

If you need help, talk to a close friend, teacher, parent, minister, or school counselor.

Use the following worksheet to help you think about how much time and energy you spend in each of the life roles you now have. Divide the circle into slices—like a pie. Make one slice for each of your roles. Make the pieces large or small based on how much time and energy you give to that role. For example, you may spend 14 hours each week practicing the piano. You may spend only 7 hours each week doing something with your family. If so, the piece of pie for "piano player" would be twice as big as the piece for "family member."

After you complete the worksheet, think about these questions:

* Which of my life roles takes up the largest amount of time and energy?

* What does this tell me about my priorities?

* Could I do a better job balancing the roles that are important to me?

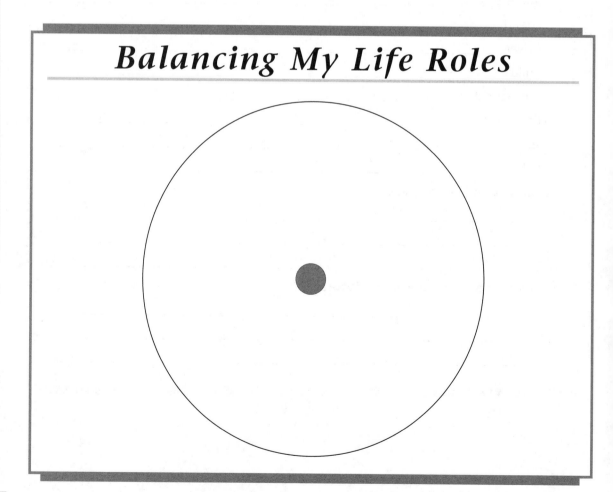

Balancing My Life Roles

You have looked at your past, current, and future roles and how you balance your roles. Complete the following worksheet. Think about how your life roles affect your career decisions.

My Roles and Decisions

Roles that give me experience and help me develop new skills: _____
_____
_____

Roles that help me reach my education and career goals: _____
_____
_____

Roles that make it hard for me to plan my education and career: _____
_____
_____

Changes I would like to make in the roles I now have: _____
_____
_____

I am satisfied with these aspects of my current balance of roles: _____
_____
_____

Roles I have now that may affect my goals and dreams for the future: _____
_____
_____

Roles I may have accepted without thinking about how they affect my future goals:
_____
_____

Roles I have because someone else expected me to have them: _____
_____
_____

Career Interests

You may not be looking for a job now, but someday you will be. Your career interests will affect your educational decisions. If you want to be happy (and who doesn't?), find an occupation that interests you. JIST Works publishes a book called *Guide for Occupational Exploration (GOE)*. This book is probably available in your school or public library. The book is based on information from the U.S. Department of Labor. For each job, the *GOE* provides information such as job duties, personality type needed, projected growth, physical and work conditions, required level of training and education, average salary, and skills required.

The *GOE's* 14 interest areas are shown on the following worksheet. Follow these instructions:

- Read each description.
- Check any that interest you.
- Select the three interest areas you find most interesting.
- Put *1* next to the area that interests you most, *2* by the next most interesting, and *3* by your third choice.

My Career Interests

My main interests are in the following areas.

_____ **Arts, Entertainment, and Media.** I am interested in expressing my feelings and ideas creatively. I am interested in communicating news and information. I am interested in performing.

_____ **Science, Math, and Engineering.** I am interested in researching and analyzing scientific, mathematical, engineering, and technological information. I am interested in applying what I know to problems in the real world, the environment, world societies, medicine, and the life and natural sciences. I am interested in working with and manipulating data. I am interested in using technology and computers.

_____ **Plants and Animals.** I am interested in working with plants and animals, usually outdoors.

_____ **Law, Law Enforcement, and Public Safety.** I am interested in protecting people. I am interested in protecting people's rights and property. I am interested in using authority and in inspecting or monitoring.

_____ **Mechanics, Installers, and Repairers.** I am interested in mechanical, electrical, or electronic principles. I am interested in using machines or hand tools.

_____ **Construction, Mining, and Drilling.** I am interested in buildings and other structures. I am interested in using mechanical devices to drill or excavate.

_____ **Transportation.** I am interested in operations that move people or materials.

_____ **Industrial Production.** I am interested in repetitive, concrete, organized activities. I am interested in working in a factory.

_____ **Business Detail.** I am interested in organized, clearly defined activities. I am interested in being accurate. I am interested in details. I am interested in working in an office.

_____ **Sales and Marketing.** I am interested in persuading people to purchase something. I am interested in selling and promoting a product or service.

_____ **Recreation, Travel, and Other Services.** I am interested in meeting the personal needs of other people. I am interested in providing travelers with cleanliness, good food and drinks, recreation, and a comfortable place to stay.

_____ **Education and Social Service.** I am interested in teaching people. I am interested in helping people improve their social or spiritual well-being.

_____ **General Management and Support.** I am interested in making an organization run smoothly.

_____ **Medical and Health Services.** I am interested in helping people be healthy.

After you think about these job interest areas, start thinking about specific jobs. Your librarian can help you find books that list jobs. You should also look at the list of jobs compiled by the U.S. Department of Labor (DOL). This list appears in a book called the *Occupational Outlook Handbook (OOH)*. Check with your teacher or your school librarian to see where you can get a copy of this book.

Look at the list of jobs in the *OOH* or in some other source. Then complete the following worksheet.

Jobs That Interest Me

Jobs I could get with the skills and knowledge I have now

_____

_____

_____

_____

Jobs that interest me but that would require additional training, education, or experience

_____

_____

_____

_____

WHAT'S NEXT?

In this chapter, you thought about what is important to you, how you learn, and what your personality is like. You looked at how you manage your life. You considered your life roles and your career interests.

In Chapter 4, you will look at your skills, experience, and education. The information will help you think about what you have to offer an interviewer.

What You Have to Offer

In Chapter 3, you focused on understanding who you are. The next step is to think about what you have to offer a prospective interviewer. This chapter will help you answer these questions:

- What work and life experience do I have that would be of interest to an interviewer?

- What have I accomplished at school, in my life, and at work?

- What skills and attributes have I developed?

- What education and training have I received?

- What do other people say about my knowledge, skills, performance, and accomplishments?

You may want to include the worksheets in this chapter in your portfolio. You can include them wherever you think they fit best. Think about how you are organizing your portfolio. Refer to Chapter 1 to review the three types of organization described there.

The worksheets are for your reference only. They are not designed to be shown to interviewers.

Work History

As you build your portfolio, you may think you should only include jobs you were paid for. If so, you underestimate what you have to offer. You have developed skills and built experiences from every part of your life, both work related and non-work related.

> You have developed skills and built experiences from every part of your life.

Jobs

Many high school students have only had one job. But you may have had more. If you've already had three or more jobs, make several copies of the following worksheet before you complete it. Then you can record information about all of your jobs. (You have the publisher's permission to make as many copies of this worksheet as you need.) If you don't have access to a copy machine, you can use the worksheet as a guide and write your job information on separate sheets of paper.

> Interviewers prefer to talk to people who know what you can do and who have worked with you at school or on the job.

Also, you may not have any paid work experience. That's okay. You can still read the information in this section and think about how it might apply to you in the future.

For each of your current and past jobs, complete a worksheet with information about your employer and your job. Tell what your responsibilities were in each job. Write as much about your job duties as possible. This will help you decide which tasks were your most important.

Also, for each job, think of someone who could serve as a reference for you. Remember that interviewers prefer to talk to people who know what you can do. They want the opinions of people who have worked with you at school or on the job. You might list a teacher, minister, or former employer. Think of people who have firsthand knowledge of your skills and strengths. Interviewers do not think references from friends and family are reliable.

Before you use people as references, be sure to ask them if it is okay. Then they won't be caught off-guard when an interviewer calls. Let your references know what kind of information you want them to share.

Include the following worksheets in your portfolio. You can then refer to them when you are filling out job or college applications or talking to an interviewer.

My Paid Employment

Job title: _____

Name of employer/organization/contact person:_____

_____

Employer's phone: _____ Employer's fax: _____

Employer's street address: _____

City/State/ZIP:_____

_____

Dates: _____

What I did: _____

_____

_____

_____

Person who could provide a reference for me related to this job: _____

_____

Person's address: _____

_____

Person's phone/fax: _____

Job title: _____

Name of employer/organization/contact person:_____

_____

Employer's phone: _____ Employer's fax: _____

Employer's street address: _____

City/State/ZIP:_____

_____

Dates: _____

What I did: _____

_____

_____

_____

Person who could provide a reference for me related to this job: _____

_____

Person's address: _____

_____

Person's phone/fax: _____

Nonwork Experience

As a student, many of your activities will not involve a job. What you do in your nonwork time can help you decide what education or career you would like.

The activities you choose to do around your home, for your community, and for other people are things you want to do. These activities can help you develop the skills interviewers look for. Be ready to show interviewers what you have learned or accomplished in these nonwork activities. Include examples, photographs, programs, or other materials in your portfolio.

> What you do in your nonwork time can help you decide what education or career you would like.

On the following worksheet, list your nonwork activities. Examples of nonwork activities include serving on a school committee, teaching a class at your church, participating in political functions, working with a youth sport team, or organizing community projects. Complete the statements in the worksheet. Check the activities you could do for pay.

My Nonwork Experience

I have been involved in many activities not related to work. I've listed some of them below. I've also placed a check mark beside the activities I think I could do in a job.

	This is something I could do in my job
At school, I do the following:	
_____	_____
_____	_____
_____	_____
_____	_____
At home, I do the following:	
_____	_____
_____	_____
_____	_____
In my spare time, I do these activities:	
_____	_____
_____	_____
_____	_____
In my community, I am active in the following:	
_____	_____
_____	_____
_____	_____

© JIST Works   *Creating Your High School Portfolio*

Accomplishments

 Focus on what you have done that makes you proud. Don't underestimate the importance of what you have accomplished.

You have done something that gave you a great sense of accomplishment. Right? Maybe it was something you did several years ago. Maybe it was something you did yesterday. Maybe you did something big. Or maybe you did something small. You may or may not have received recognition, but what you did mattered to you.

Looking at what you have accomplished can help you identify your skills. You are probably good at and enjoy using these skills. If you find a school or job that lets you use your skills, you will be happier.

As you consider your education and career plans, avoid focusing on your failures. Instead, focus on what you have done that makes you proud. This will build your self-confidence. It will help you identify skills and abilities that will interest future employers.

Don't underestimate the importance of what you have accomplished. Think about your experiences. Look for the skills you have developed. For example:

- Maybe you helped your friends do something. If so, you may have learned to work as part of a team. You may have developed problem-solving skills.

- Maybe you are involved in activities at your place of worship. If so, you have probably developed people skills. You may have learned to take responsibility and be dependable.

- Maybe you have had a summer job. If so, you probably know how to budget your money. You probably know how to stay organized and manage your time.

- Maybe you have worked at staying physically fit and healthy. If so, you probably have a lot of energy. You are probably disciplined and motivated.

As you complete the following worksheet, list accomplishments and activities you are proud of. Consider all your life experiences.

My Accomplishments

Three things I've done that I am really proud of are

1. _____

_____

2. _____

_____

3. _____

_____

Skills and Attributes

No matter what you do during or after high school, you need to know what your skills are. Then when you meet with an interviewer, you can emphasize your most valuable skills. You can communicate what you have done and how well you did it.

> A skill is simply something you can do well. You probably have hundreds of skills, not just a few.

Many people think their job title describes their abilities. They think they don't have any skills if they don't have a job. As a student, you may think interviewers will have this attitude. The truth is that interviewers are not just interested in job skills. They look for skills related to your personality. They look for skills that will make you a good student or worker. These skills are often called transferable skills. They can be transferred from one job to another.

In the book *The Quick Job Search: Seven Steps to Getting a Good Job in Less Time,* published by JIST Works, author Michael Farr identifies three types of skills:

- **Self-Management Skills.** These are skills that are part of your basic personality. These skills give you the ability to adapt to new situations. These skills are an indication of the kind of student or worker you will be. Flexibility, friendliness, and punctuality are examples of self-management skills.

- **Transferable Skills.** These are skills that can be used in various jobs or educational programs. They may be learned in one job or in your life experiences. But they can be used in other situations, too. Meeting deadlines and writing clearly are examples of transferable skills.

- **Job-Related Skills.** These are the skills you need to do one certain job. These skills would not be required in most jobs, but they would be essential in certain jobs. Being able to drive a truck, prepare a teaching plan, or interpret a heart monitor are examples of job-related skills.

If you need additional help to identify your skills, visit your library or a bookstore. Talk with friends, teachers, and family. Ask these people what they think are your most important skills.

Remember that a skill is simply something you do well. You probably have hundreds of skills, not just a few.

Also, remember that there is a difference between what you do and what you **can** do. For example, right now you may not know how to cut someone's hair. But you could do it after someone teaches you how.

The skills you have make you a unique individual. Your skills will change over time. Some skills will continue to develop more than others.

The following table illustrates how you might document certain skills in your portfolio.

Skill	How I demonstrate this skill	What I can include in my portfolio
Self-management	I'm always on time for work.	My job review
Negotiation	I wrote a chores contract for my family.	Copy of the family contract
Organization	I helped plan and organize the school dance.	Copies of my letters or memos to other committee members

If you have trouble thinking of what to include in your portfolio, talk to a friend, family member, or teacher who can help you.

Refer to the previous table as you complete the following worksheet. Place check marks beside the skills you have. Think how you have demonstrated those skills. Then think about what you can include in your portfolio that would document that skill. If you are not familiar with a word used in the worksheet, look it up in a dictionary.

In your portfolio, include the documentation that shows that you have these skills.

My Skills—Demonstrated and Documented

Skill	How I Demonstrate This Skill	What I Can Include in My Portfolio
_____ Communication	_____	_____
_____ Computer knowledge	_____	_____
_____ Writing	_____	_____
_____ Decision making	_____	_____
_____ Dependability	_____	_____
_____ Initiative	_____	_____
_____ Integrity/honesty	_____	_____
_____ Knowing how to learn	_____	_____
_____ Creativity	_____	_____
_____ Cooperation	_____	_____
_____ Critical thinking	_____	_____
_____ Leadership	_____	_____
_____ Analysis	_____	_____
_____ Listening	_____	_____
_____ Persistence	_____	_____
_____ Problem solving	_____	_____
_____ Reading	_____	_____
_____ Mathematics	_____	_____
_____ Sociability	_____	_____
_____ Teamwork	_____	_____
_____ Speaking	_____	_____
_____ Reasoning	_____	_____
_____ Self-esteem	_____	_____
_____ Self-management	_____	_____
_____ Tolerance	_____	_____
_____ Job-related skills such as cooking, keyboarding, or doing yard work	_____	_____

Education and Training

In the Education and Training section of your portfolio, you can include information about

- Your grades (transcripts)
- Apprenticeships
- Internships
- Certificates
- Diplomas
- Favorite school subjects
- Courses completed
- General Educational Development certificate (GED)
- Languages
- Licenses
- Military training
- On-the-job training
- Things you have taught yourself
- Volunteer service
- Workshops
- Special interests

> This section of your portfolio can include anything that shows what you've learned in school or from someone else.

You can include anything that shows what you've learned in school or from someone else. It might include what you have done on the job. It might include what you have done in your home or community. It might be something you did just for yourself.

People's Opinions

 Tip Sharing good feedback from other people is not bragging.

Review your experiences. Include in your portfolio any awards, letters of recognition, performance evaluations, and positive comments by teachers, employers, community leaders, coaches, or ministers.

You may hesitate to include these good things in your portfolio. You may feel that you are bragging. However, sharing good feedback from other people is not bragging. Keep any documents you have that indicate you have done something that made a difference in someone's work or life.

Life Changes

One sure fact of life is that things constantly change. You have undoubtedly experienced and managed many changes in your life. These changes might include

- Going to school for the first time
- Changing schools
- Moving
- Being away from home
- Taking your first job
- Starting or ending a friendship

> If you want to improve your life in any way, you will have to make some changes.

How do you feel about change? Many people do not like it. It means you have to let go of the familiar and move toward the unknown. However, change can be a healthy challenge. If you want to improve your life in any way, you will have to make some changes.

Overcoming Fear

When you think about making a change, you may have some fear about what will happen. Carole Kanchier wrote a book called *Dare to Change Your Job and Your Life*. In the book, Ms. Kanchier says that

- Fear can keep you from making a change
- Fear is a barrier you have to go through
- Growing means you have to leave a situation you are comfortable with
- Growing is painful
- People try to think of ways to avoid pain
- Trying to avoid pain may make you decide not to make any changes
- You should admit that you have some fears about changing

> Fear can keep you from making a change.

If you know what you are afraid of, you can deal with your fears openly and honestly. You can learn to face change without fear. Taking action to overcome your barriers is the first step. Use the following worksheet to help you think about the changes in your life and how you handle such changes.

I Make Changes

Two things I fear or dislike about change are

1. _____

   _____

2. _____

   _____

Two things that excite me about change are

1. _____

   _____

2. _____

   _____

Two things I have learned about myself from the changes I've faced are

1. _____

   _____

2. _____

   _____

Overcoming Life's Barriers

Have you noticed that when you succeed at something, you have more confidence to try again? You have already accomplished many things. You have also probably experienced setbacks. But have you ever thought that these setbacks can be good learning experiences?

Life doesn't stand still. It changes. The economy changes. Industries and employment opportunities change. Jobs come and go. You can choose to stand still and be left behind. Or you can choose to grow and pursue new opportunities.

Sometimes you face barriers you can't change. If so, you have to make other choices. But sometimes you may be overlooking the possibilities. You may be able to overcome a barrier if you think creatively.

You may have circumstances in your life that hold you back. These circumstances are barriers. They can keep you from reaching your goals. They can keep you from making the changes you want to make. Creating your portfolio makes you aware of barriers you may be facing. It also helps you see what your options are.

You may not feel free to make all the choices you would like to make. You may feel that certain things limit your options. Sometimes these are things you can't change. If so, you have to make other choices. But sometimes you may be overlooking the possibilities. You may be able to overcome a barrier if you think creatively.

Do you feel that certain barriers are keeping you from making the changes you want to make? Ask yourself these questions:

- Did I help create this barrier?

- Is the situation really beyond my control?

- Can I change my way of thinking about the barrier?

- Are there ways around this barrier that I haven't considered?

On the following worksheet, check the items that could be barriers for you. Next, briefly describe what you could do to overcome that barrier. For example, you may want to enroll in a technical training program. But you may not have the money you need to get started. Your lack of money is a barrier. But you can overcome this barrier. You could work full time for a year or two after high school to save enough money to enroll. Improving your life may take time. But you will eventually be successful.

My Personal Barriers

The items I checked below are my personal barriers. I've described what I might be able to do to overcome each barrier.

_____ Transportation _____

_____

_____ Budget _____

_____

_____ Education _____

_____

_____ Appearance/clothing _____

_____

_____ Family responsibilities _____

_____

_____ Gender _____

_____

_____ Other _____

_____

_____

_____

© JIST Works

You now have some ideas about what you can do to remove the barriers in your life. Ask other people to comment on your barriers. Write down every suggestion, even the ones that sound silly or impossible. Sometimes a silly-sounding idea may lead you to a solution. When you think your list is complete, pick one or two ideas and try them.

You may decide that your barriers are too great for you to overcome by yourself. If so, talk to a teacher or counselor who can help you. You may have trouble making changes or accepting your limitations. If so, look for books, magazines, and other resources that can help you.

Remember that making changes can be overwhelming. Don't try to change your life all at once.

WHAT'S NEXT?

In this chapter, you learned how to show an interviewer what you can do and what you know. You thought about what items to include in your portfolio.

In Chapter 5, you will get information that will help you reach your career goals. You will begin exploring career options.

Part Three

Reaching Your Career Goals

Chapter 5

Exploring Career Options

In this book, you have learned to organize and use your portfolio. You have also increased your understanding of who you are and what you have to offer. This chapter will help you answer the following questions:

- How can I keep track of information about careers?
- What kind of job would be the perfect job for me?
- Where can I find career information?
- Where can I find information about a specific job?
- Would I like to be self-employed someday?

In your portfolio, you can include the worksheets and checklists in this chapter. These are not items you would want to show to an employer, but they will serve as valuable references as you look for a job.

Gathering Career Information

You may already be making decisions about your future education and career. If not, you soon will be. You need

> Keep track of what you find out about various careers. Refer to several sources.

- A basic understanding of your options
- Information about the positive and negative aspects of each option

Do you plan to start your career right after high school? Do you plan to get additional training or education after high school? In either case, you need career information. When you are exploring careers, you will gather information about specific jobs and occupations. For example

- The nature of the work
- The industries that include these occupations
- Training or education required
- Working conditions
- Employment trends and advancement possibilities
- Related occupations
- How well your values, interests, education, skills, and abilities match

Keep track of what you find out about various careers. Refer to several sources. Look for information about

- Employment trends
- Occupations and industries that are growing
- Job openings now and in the future

Use the following worksheet to track information about a certain occupation. You may not be able to complete the worksheet now. But you should be able to complete it after you finish this chapter.

Make photocopies of the following worksheet. Make a copy for each occupation that interests you. Refer to Chapter 3 to find job titles that interest you.

My Career Research

Name of occupation: _____

Source of information: _____

What I would be expected to do:_____

_____

_____

The risks of this kind of work: _____

_____

_____

The physical demands of this career: _____

_____

_____

Skills I would need: Do I have this skill?

_____   _____

_____   _____

_____   _____

How much work I would be expected to do at one time:_____

_____

How fast I would have to do the work: _____

_____

What I would see, hear, or smell in this job: _____

_____

People in this job work _____ hours per day.

People in this job work _____ days per week.

People in this job work _____ hours of overtime per week.

People in this job travel _____ days per year.

Training and education required for this job: _____

_____

Licenses, registrations, or certificates required: _____

_____

How much money people make in this job: _____

_____

Number of job openings this career is expected to have: _____

_____

Potential for advancement or promotions: _____

_____

_____

Related occupations: _____

_____

_____

Where I can get more information about this career (books, school, people): _____

_____

_____

The Perfect Job for You

Before you begin looking at career options, think about what would be the perfect job for you. Think about the job that you've always wanted. Think about a job that would meet most of your needs. Also, think about what you know about yourself.

Few people find a job that is ideal in every way. But the more you focus on what you want, the closer you will get to finding your ideal job. As you complete the following worksheet, imagine yourself in your perfect or ideal job.

> Few people find a job that is ideal in every way. But the more you focus on what you want, the closer you will get to finding your ideal job.

My Perfect Job

Location

In my perfect job, I would stay in the United States.   ____ yes   ____ no

The region of the country I would work in is _____

_____

In my ideal job, I would work in a foreign country.   ____ yes   ____ no

The climate where my ideal job is would be _____

_____

The size of city I would work in is _____

I would work in   ____ an urban setting   ____ a rural setting

Work Site

In my ideal job I would work   ____ inside ____ outside

I would work for   _____ a big company   _____ a small company

I would   _____ stay in one place   _____ move around

In my ideal job I would want to wear clothes that are_____

_____

My ideal work site would have some kind of equipment in it.   ____ yes ____ no

Tasks and Responsibilities

My ideal job would involve

_____ physical tasks

_____ mental tasks

_____ a combination

The amount of time I would spend working with data and information: _____

The amount of time I would spend working with people: _____

The number of people I would work with: _____

The amount of time I would spend working with equipment: _____

_____

I would be   ____ a leader   ____ a follower

I would be   ____ a planner   ____ a doer

The skills I would use in my ideal job:_____

_____

During a typical work day, I would _____

_____

Coworkers

In my ideal job, I would have a boss who is _____

_____

I would be the boss or supervisor.   ____ yes   ____ no

I would be part of a team.   ____ yes   ____ no

The number of people working with me would be _____

_____

My coworkers in my ideal job could be described as _____

_____

I would work alone.   ____ yes   ____ no

Sources of Career Information

Lots of information about careers is available. Sometimes you may feel overloaded. Making a career decision will be easier if you know what would be the perfect job for you.

You can get information from

- Newspapers and magazines
- Television and radio
- Your friends and teachers
- Your high school classes
- The Internet

> Do not disregard a major career interest because you uncovered some negative information. Continue exploring all your interests.

Consider the information you get. Ask yourself these questions:

- **Is the information up to date?** A survey that was taken five years ago is not as reliable as a survey that was taken this year. Things change. Career information quickly gets out of date. Be sure you know when the information was gathered.

- **Is the information accurate?** Some information passes through many sources. It can become slanted. It can be misinterpreted. It can even be completely wrong. Be sure the information is not just someone's opinion.

- **Is the information unbiased?** Sometimes a person or organization presents only part of the available information. This makes the information seem to support the person's or organization's view. Be sure the career information you gather is complete and objective.

- **Is the information confirmed by other sources?** When you find career information, see if you can find the same information somewhere else. For example, you might talk to five people about the same career. You might receive the same information from all five people. If so, you can probably rely on that information.

You will consider many careers. And you will uncover negative information about almost every career. Don't give up on any career that interests you. Continue exploring all your interests. Keep looking for information until you have everything you need.

Let's look at some tools you can use to explore career options.

Informational Interviews

You probably know what a job interview is. But have you ever heard of an informational interview? An informational interview is just what it sounds like it would be. It is an interview in which you gather career information.

The purpose of an informational interview is to gain information, not to interview for a job. You can request an informational interview with someone who works in a career area that interests you.

The following worksheet lists questions you can ask at an informational interview. You can also write some of your own questions. Be sure your questions will help you get the information you need. Do not ask questions that are too personal. For example, you should not ask specific questions about the person's salary.

> An informational interview is one in which you gather career information. The purpose is to gain information, not to interview for a job.

My Informational Interviews

General Questions to Ask

Preparation

- What education or training is required?
- What experience do I need?
- How did **you** prepare for this kind of work or education?

Present Job

- What do you do during a typical week?
- What takes up most of your time at work?
- What skills do you need for doing your job?
- How would you describe your work environment?
- What are the toughest problems you deal with on a day-to-day basis?
- What do you find most rewarding about your job?

Lifestyle

- Does your situation limit your personal time or where you can live?
- How are you expected to dress at work?
- How many hours are you expected to spend at work each week?
- Do you get vacation time and other benefits?

Career Future and Alternatives

- What do you hope to achieve in the future?
- Do you think there will be job opportunities in the future for people to do what you are doing now?
- If you had to change jobs, what else might you do?
- What companies hire people with your background?

Job Hunting

- How do people find out about jobs in your career area? Are jobs advertised in the newspaper or professional journals? Is information passed by word of mouth?
- How does a person move from one position to another in this type work?
- When you hire someone, what characteristics do you look for? Why?

Education	Knowledge of the organization
Personality	Knowledge of the job
Work experience	Other

continues

continued

Advice

- Do you think I have what it takes to be successful in this career?
- Can you suggest other schools or related jobs that might be better for me?
- What types of paid employment or other experience are important for me to have?
- If you were my age, would you do anything differently in choosing a career? What school courses would you take? What kind of experience would you try to get?

Referral to Others

- Do you know of other people who could provide me with information?
- Can you suggest a few people who might be willing to see me?
- May I use your name when I contact the people you suggest?

Job-Specific Questions

- What does your organization do?
- How big is your company?
- In what other cities does your company have offices?
- How much freedom is given to new employees?
- How long do people usually stay with your company?
- What types of formal or on-the-job training does your organization provide?
- How do employees transfer from one position to another within the company?
- What new product lines or services is the company developing?
- Is your company growing?
- How does the company compare to other companies?

Job Shadowing

Another way to get career information is to do job shadowing. When you job shadow, you go to work with someone for a day, a few days, or even a week to observe all aspects of the person's occupation. This allows you to see firsthand what a person in a job really does.

> Job shadowing allows you to see firsthand what a person in a job really does.

Job Clubs

You can find job clubs in community or government agencies. Job clubs teach people how to look for work. They also teach people how to locate and contact employers. The leaders and members of these clubs can provide you with emotional support and encouragement.

Career Information Systems

Contact your school or public library to see what kinds of computer support is available to you. Many software programs can match information about you to possible careers. These programs also provide information about job duties, skills, training or education, pay, and related jobs.

Career Resource Centers

Career resource centers provide many sources of information in one place. Check with nearby businesses, technical schools, and colleges. Libraries and government or community agencies may also have career centers. You can find information in books or magazines or on videos and DVDs.

The Internet

Start with government sites such as http://online.onetcenter.org. Another option is www.jist.com.

Networking

The term *network* refers to all the connections you have with people and information. Networking is the way most people find jobs. And networking is not difficult. You already know many people. The people you know also know many people. These people are all part of your network.

The purpose of networking is to get information that can lead you to a job. The people in your network can give you job information. They can also serve as references for you.

> You already know many people. The people you know also know many people. These people are all part of your network.

Ask the people in your network if they know of any jobs. Tell them what you do, what you do well, and what you want to do.

Start your network with your family. Then, go to your friends. Contact people you have worked for or with. Talk to people you meet while doing volunteer work at school or in your community. They may know someone who could give you career information.

Some people will tell you they don't know anyone who can help you. They're probably thinking only in terms of people who could actually give you a job. Explain to them what you are looking for. A person may not know anyone who can help you directly. But they may know someone who knows someone else who can help you.

© JIST Works

You will meet new people while you are exploring careers. Add these people's names to your network. Get their telephone numbers. When you talk with someone about career options, ask them if they can recommend others who might help you.

Ask each person you know to give you the names and phone numbers of three people who might be able to help you. Contact those people. Ask them for the names and numbers of three more people. You will soon have a large network that can help you find the information you want.

Always send thank-you notes to people in your network who give you job information. Collect business cards, flyers, and brochures from people and businesses that interest you. Store these materials in your portfolio.

After you decide on a career, let the people in your network know. Ask them if they know of a job in that career field. After you get a job, contact these people again. Tell them about your new job. Thank them for their help.

Figure 1 on this page is a visual picture of a person's network.

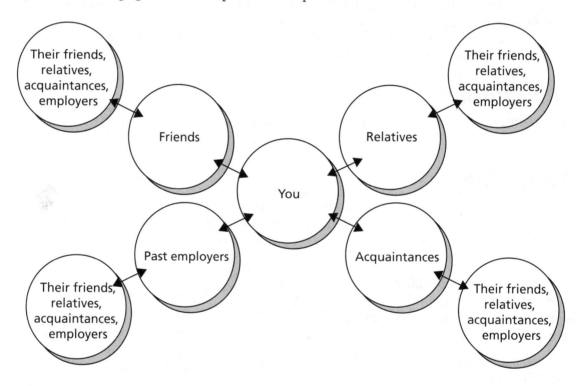

Figure 1. Diagram of a person's network.

Look at the following figure. Record information about your own network. Add more pages if you need to. Use actual names of people wherever possible. Fill in the information about your own network.

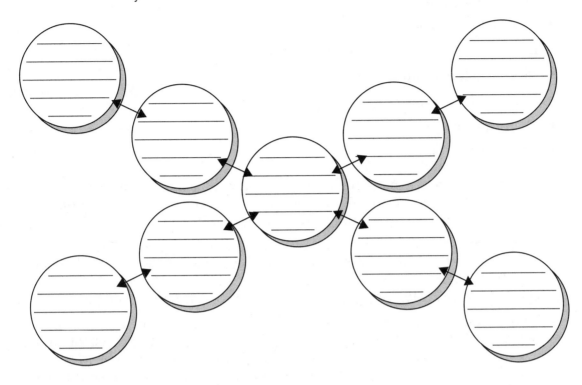

Figure 2. Diagram of your network.

Training Options

Tip

If you have good education and training, you will have an easier time finding a job that interests you. You will also make more money than someone with less education.

Some days you may get tired of being in school. But remember that the education, training, and experience you receive during and after high school are important. If you have good education and training:

- You will have an easier time finding a job that interests you.
- You will make more money than someone with less education.

So, where can you find out what your education and training options are? Consider these sources:

- Armed forces processing center
- High school guidance office
- Human resources department of a company
- Nearby college or university
- State employment office
- Technical college
- The Internet

As you can see, there are many training options available. Some last only a short time. Others may take a year or more. You will learn more about these training options in Chapter 7. Keep the following ideas in mind:

- Employers sometimes recruit from certain training programs and not others. Talk to at least one or two employers before you enroll in a training program for after high school. Ask the employers what they think of the program you are considering. Ask whether they would hire someone from that program.

- Tuition and fees vary from one school to another. So does the training you receive. Call several programs to compare their quality and cost. Ask questions like these: What time of day do classes meet? How long would I be in the program? Would I get credit for my work experience? Can I take courses through the mail or online?

- Most schools are certified by a national organization. This includes public and private schools. It includes colleges and trade schools. The national organization sets standards that the schools are expected to meet. The organization determines if the school offers good-quality training. When you contact a school, ask if it is accredited. Ask for the name of the national organization that accredits the school. If you are in doubt, contact your state department of education.

- Most schools have financial aid programs. Special programs in your area may provide funds for training. Ask the school what is available. Find out if you qualify. If you already have a job, your employer may pay all or part of the costs of your education.

The following worksheet lists ways to improve your knowledge and training. Check those that interest you. Ask people in your network for advice. Your school librarian or counselor can help you find out what training programs are offered in your area.

I Explore Training Options

I Could Get More Training By...	Where	When
____ Reading journals or books to update my knowledge		
____ Enrolling in a trade, technical, or vocational school		
____ Enrolling in a degree program		
____ Two-year program		
____ Four-year program		
____ Masters program		
____ Other degree program		
____ Enrolling in courses offered by my employer		
____ Getting a license or certificate		
____ Joining the military		
____ Beginning an apprenticeship program		
____ Beginning a job-training program		
____ Taking a temporary job that would add to my skills		
____ Other		

Self-Employment

You are already thinking about what careers interest you. You also may want to think about someday working for yourself. The term for this is *self-employment*. Most people get great satisfaction from turning their dreams into something real.

One of the best things about self-employment is that **you** define what *success* means. Your definition of *success* depends on why you want to start your own business.

> One of the best things about self-employment is that **you** define what *success* means.

Anyone who works needs skills. People who are self-employed need skills that not everyone needs. But you can get the skills and knowledge you need. Here are two options:

- Classes are available on how to set up a small business. You may want to attend these classes.

- You may also want to take a self-employment test. You can get information from your school guidance counselor. Free assessments are available on the Internet; for example, http://www.2h.com/Tests/entrepreneur.html.

Do you think you would like to be self-employed? Research your options. Three main ways to become self-employed are to

- Start a new business based on your own idea

- Purchase an existing business from someone else

- Buy a store that is part of a chain of stores

Another way to be self-employed is to become a freelancer. Freelancers do not usually have other people working for or with them. They usually work by themselves, and they often work at home. They make contracts with various companies and employers to provide specific services or products. They usually work on short-term assignments. They may have periods when they are very busy, with several assignments. They also have periods when they have little work to do. Examples include freelance proofreaders and graphic artists.

Here are some other ideas to consider:

- Before you start your own business, you may want to work for someone else. Try to get a job in the kind of business that interests you. This will help you get the skills and experiences you need to be self-employed.

- Talk to people who own their own businesses. Ask them about their experiences, joys, problems, mistakes, and successes.

> Talk to people who own their own businesses. Ask them about their experiences, joys, problems, mistakes, and successes.

The following worksheet helps you think about your attributes. It helps you decide whether you would enjoy working for yourself. If several of the statements apply to you, you may want to consider being self-employed.

I Consider Working for Myself

The statements I checked are ones that apply to me.

____ I have a great idea for a new product or service.

____ I don't mind taking financial risks.

____ I like to work hard.

____ I like being in charge of things.

____ I like to take responsibility for my own success and failure.

____ I am creative, flexible, and open to new ideas.

____ I am a self-starter.

____ I have a lot of self-discipline.

____ I commit myself to meeting deadlines.

____ I like working alone.

____ I can do whatever it takes to get the job done.

____ I do not mind working long hours.

____ I can manage money.

____ I like setting my own schedule.

____ I can set and keep work priorities.

____ I can motivate myself and other people.

____ I work well with other people.

____ I am able to convince others about my point of view.

WHAT'S NEXT?

In this chapter, you learned how and where to get career information. You thought about your ideal job and about where to get the education you need.

In Chapter 6, you will get information about making career decisions and deciding on a career direction.

Chapter 6

Deciding on a Career Direction

You've been making decisions for a long time. Some were probably small decisions. Some were bigger. Deciding what you want to do with your life is a huge decision.

In this chapter, you will look at a step-by-step model that can help you make career decisions. The information here will help you answer these questions:

- What are the steps involved in making a career decision?

- Are my career decisions influenced by who I am?

- What sources can help me consider various careers?

- What jobs most closely match my idea of the perfect job?

- What one career decision do I want to make now?

You may want to include in your portfolio some of the worksheets in this chapter. They should be included for your reference only.

Childhood Dreams

For some people, choosing a career is difficult. For other people, it is not. Some people know at an early age what they want to do. Some people change their mind several times. Actor Raymond Burr once said,

> *"The policeman is the little boy who grew up to be what he said he was going to be."*

Think back to your childhood, when you knew very little about careers. The following worksheet will help you think about what you wanted to be when you grew up.

When I Was a Child

When I was a child, I wanted to be _____

_____

_____

I was interested in the job because _____

_____

_____

I was influenced by _____

_____

_____

_____ My decision changed over the years. Here's why.

_____

_____

_____

_____ My decision never changed. Here's why.

_____

_____

_____

© JIST Works *Creating Your High School Portfolio*

Career Decision-Making Model

You are no longer a child. You are faced with the reality of having to think about a career. There is no magic formula for making good decisions. You have to learn as you go.

People make career decisions in various ways. Some people follow the advice of other people. Some people take the first job that comes along. Other people choose an occupation because it has a lot of openings.

Sometimes people's decisions turn out well. Other times they do not. Adults sometimes wish they could just start over. If they could, many people say they would choose a different career. And they say they would definitely get more career information before making a decision.

> There is no magic formula for making good decisions. You have to learn as you go.

But you are different. You are spending time thinking about who you are and what you want. You are gathering information about possible careers.

Look at Figure 3 on this page. This figure is called a Career Decision-Making Model. It illustrates one good way to make decisions.

The wheel in Figure 3 shows what steps you should take when making decisions. Start with *decide to decide* and follow each step. This will help you achieve your career and life goals. In this chapter, you will learn more about the first six steps on the model.

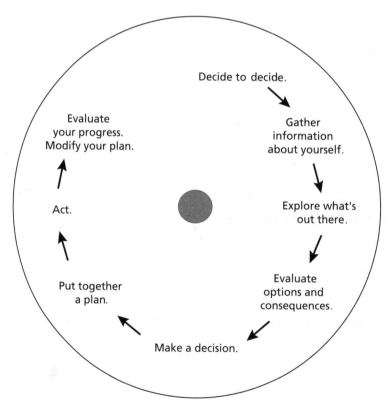

Figure 3. Career Decision-Making Model.

Decide to Decide

Tip Remember that nothing can keep you from deciding to decide.

The first step on the Career Decision-Making Model is to *decide to decide.* Many people have a habit of putting off doing things they don't want to do. They put off facing or even thinking about decisions. They may not make decisions because of conflicts they are having. They may think they just don't have time to make a good decision. They may just not want to do whatever it is they are putting off doing. But career decisions are vital. Do not put them off, even if they are hard.

Here's an example of how you might put off making a career decision. Maybe the career you want requires a two-year college degree. You are graduating from high school this year. You may think it is okay to take the summer off and to not start thinking about college until in the fall. However, the application process takes time. If you wait until the fall, you will probably miss a semester or more that you could have been in school. That time is lost and can't be recovered.

Remember that nothing can keep you from deciding to decide. Do you want to make a career decision? Do you want to find a career you will enjoy? If so, you are already motivated to take the first step—deciding to decide.

There are no right or wrong decisions. And there are no right or wrong reasons for making career decisions. Evaluate your situation. Determine what is best for you. Doing this means you have to know and listen to yourself. If you have completed the worksheets in the previous chapters of this book, you already have a good idea about who you are. Now is the time to decide what you want.

The following worksheet asks you to describe what you hope to accomplish. You may want to make extra copies of the worksheet before you write on it. Complete each sentence. Include as much information about your decision as possible.

I Decide to Decide

What career decision am I ready to make? _____

_____

_____

Why do I want to make this decision? _____

_____

_____

When do I want to see the results of my decision?_____

_____

_____

Gather Information About Yourself

The second step on the career decision-making model is to *gather information about yourself.* You have now spent a lot of time getting to know more about yourself. You may have learned something new. You may have looked at yourself in a new way. Maybe you remembered some things you knew about yourself but had forgotten. And now, you may not know what to do with all this information.

> Getting to know yourself takes a long time. Don't worry if things do not fall into place easily.

Getting to know yourself takes a long time. Don't worry if things do not fall into place easily.

> *"I wonder if I've been changed in the night? Let me think: was I the same when I got up this morning? I almost think I can remember feeling a little different. But if I'm not the same, the next question is, 'Who in the world am I?' Ah, that's the great puzzle!"*
>
> —*Lewis Carroll*, Alice's Adventures in Wonderland

Sorting It All Out

What should you do with the information you know about yourself?

- Sort it out

- Analyze it

- Determine how to apply it

> When you take a close look at yourself, you may find out that you are stronger than you thought.

All this takes time. What you know about yourself applies to every part of your life. The more you know about yourself, the better equipped you are to make good choices.

Getting to know yourself means you have to take a clear honest look at who you are. You may have a hard time being honest with yourself about certain parts of your life. Maybe these parts of your life are hard to face. Maybe they evoke unpleasant memories. Unfortunately, these issues will not go away just because you don't face them.

One way to confront difficult issues is to keep a journal. Write about the things you don't want to face. Also, talk to someone in your family, a close and trusted friend, a minister or rabbi, or a professional counselor. Remember that help is available. When you take a close look at yourself, you may find out that you are stronger than you thought.

Knowing Yourself

All decisions start with the question, "What do I want?" You have already gathered information about yourself. This information includes what you value and what you have to offer in terms of skills and experiences.

> All decisions start with the question, "What do I want?"

Also, you have already thought about the barriers that can keep you from reaching your goals. You have examined your work and life achievements.

If you have a job now or if you have had a job before, take time now to review your work history. Use the following worksheet. In the first column, list your job titles and a brief description of each job. In the other two columns, list what you liked and disliked about each job.

Even if you have never had a job, become familiar with this worksheet. It can be a reminder to you about the things you think you would like and dislike about certain kinds of work.

My Likes and Dislikes

	What I Liked	**What I Disliked**
Current or most recent position:		
Previous position:		
Position prior to that:		

Explore What's Out There

The third step of the Career Decision-Making Model is to *explore what's out there*. If you want to make good career decisions, you need to know what opportunities are available.

> If you want to make good career decisions, you need to know what opportunities are available.

Chapter 5 gave you information about exploring careers. You probably have careers in mind that you would like to explore further. Don't underestimate the value of up-to-date, reliable career information.

© JIST Works

Creating Your High School Portfolio

One organization that provides good labor market information is the Bureau of Labor Statistics, U.S. Department of Labor (DOL). This government agency publishes bulletins, articles, periodicals, and books that tell what is going on in the world of work. Think about how certain trends may affect your situation positively or negatively. Here are some trends reflected in the DOL's most recent *Occupational Outlook Handbook:*

- Education and earnings are related. Many jobs do not require a college degree. However, jobs that pay more require either training beyond high school or years of work experience.

- Knowledge of computer and other technologies is increasingly important. People without job-related technical and computer skills will have a difficult time finding good opportunities.

- Ongoing education and training are essential. All employees are expected to improve their skills. People without technical or computer skills must get them.

- Good career-planning and job-seeking skills are more important than ever. Most people change jobs many times. Most people make major career changes five to seven times.

This information from the Department of Labor is just general information. You must decide how to apply it to your situation.

Evaluate Options and Consequences

 Tip Learn as much as you can about each action or decision you consider.

The fourth step of the Career Decision-Making Model (page 86) is to *evaluate options and consequences.* Every action you take has consequences. Every decision you make has consequences. Sometimes the consequences are negative. For example, you might hit a baseball and break a window. Sometimes the consequences are positive. For example, you might hit a baseball and score a home run.

You cannot predict every consequence for every action or decision. Many consequences are beyond your control. But if you think before you act, you are more likely to get positive consequences.

Learn as much as you can about each action or decision you consider. Think about possible outcomes. Decide if you can live with the possible bad results. Think about what you can do to be sure the results are good.

Remember this: You may not have control of every situation. But you do have control of your attitudes and reactions. You can choose to have a positive attitude or a negative attitude toward any consequence.

You also have at least some control over your circumstances. You can see that you have many choices and options. Now you need to sort through your options. You will eliminate some options and focus on others. This is one of the most difficult parts of making a decision. The following Career Options Grid gives you a place to start.

Career Options Grid

This grid will help you compare information about yourself to information about careers. As you complete the following worksheet, ask yourself these questions about your career options:

- Does this career involve doing things that interest me?
- Does this career require skills I have or would like to develop?
- Is the work schedule and environment suitable for me?
- Do I have the training or education I need?
- Will this career provide the money I need?
- How many new jobs will be available in this career?
- Does this career match my values and personality?
- Does this career match my physical and mental abilities?
- Does this career match the picture I have for my future?

Look at the following worksheet. Here's how the grid works:

1. On the left side of the grid are work and personal characteristics.

2. The first column at the top is labeled "Ideal Job." In this column, every work and personal characteristic is checked. This is to show that your ideal job would be what you are looking for in each area.

3. In the other five columns across the top, list five careers you are considering.

4. In the column below each career, check the aspects of the career that match those of your ideal job.

5. Put a slash (/) in the box, if the option is only partly compatible with what you want.

6. Leave the space blank if the option doesn't fit at all.

My Career Options Grid

Work Characteristics	Ideal Job	Option 1:	Option 2:	Option 3:	Option 4:	Option 5:
Advancement	X					
Coworkers	X					
Earnings	X					
Future	X					
Location	X					
Physical demands	X					
Responsibilities	X					
Risks	X					
Tasks	X					
Work environment	X					
Work load	X					
Work pace	X					
Work schedule	X					

Personal Characteristics

Accomplishments	X					
Career values	X					
Decision-making style	X					
Education and training	X					
Emotional health	X					
Learning style	X					
Life roles	X					
Life values	X					
Nonwork experience	X					
Personality style	X					
Physical health	X					
Risk-taking style	X					
Skills	X					
Stress-management style	X					
Time-management style	X					
Work experience	X					

Reviewing Your Career Options Grid

Review what you checked under each career. Think about how well each career matches your work and personal characteristics. Decide what is most important to you. Are earnings more important than having coworkers you like? Is having a good work schedule more important than getting to use your skills? Which options suit you best?

Put a check mark beside the two careers you think suit you best.

Think about what might happen if you choose one of those two careers. What consequences might you face? Can you live with those consequences? How would your decision change your life? Think of both positive and negative outcomes. Determine which positive and negative consequences are most important to you.

On the following worksheet, list the two career options you chose as the best match for you. Refer to the Career Options Grid. Use words, pictures, or symbols to describe the positive and negative things that may happen as a result of your decisions.

My Top Two Career Choices

Of the careers I've considered, the two I think most closely match my idea of the perfect job are

1. _____

2. _____

Some possible positive and negative consequences of these two options are

1. _____

_____

_____

_____

_____

2. _____

_____

_____

_____

_____

Make a Decision

You have completed the first four steps of the Career Decision-Making Model. The fifth step is to *make a decision.*

> **Y**ou don't have to map out your whole life right now. You can just think about the next few years.

Making a decision is difficult. You can think of all kinds of possibilities. But just thinking about the possibilities doesn't make them a reality.

Evaluating your decisions is an important part of the process. Don't overlook it. You are the only person who can determine whether your decisions are good or bad ones.

Make a commitment to your decisions. Follow through on them. Prioritize your activities. Be sure your career comes out on top.

Don't just look at the big picture. Break big goals down into a series of smaller goals. Focus your energies on what you decide to do.

Be aware of how you feel after you make your decision. Are you excited about the possibilities that await you? Are you scared? Are you relieved? Are you confident?

Remember that feeling concerned or scared doesn't mean you made the wrong choice. Those feelings are normal. However, if you are feeling more anxiety than contentment, you may want to review the information under "Self-Management Style" in Chapter 3.

Also, remember that no decision is final. You can always change your mind and revise your decision. But don't give up on your decision too quickly. In time, your feelings of concern or uncertainty may change to feelings of confidence and happiness.

If you have trouble deciding what you want, don't feel bad. You don't have to map out your whole life right now. You can just think about the next few years.

In the following worksheet, indicate what career you plan to pursue. Refer to the previous worksheet called "My Top Two Career Choices" on page 93. Consider personal reasons and outside factors. Think about your feelings, your likes and dislikes, and the information you have about the career. Record your best career option and the reasons you think this is the best choice for you.

My Decision

I have completed the worksheets titled "My Career Options Grid" (page 92) and "My Top Two Career Choices" (page 93). The career I plan to pursue is

_____

My reasons for choosing this career are _____

_____

_____

My feelings about making this decision are _____

_____

_____

Put Together a Plan

Keep in mind that there is no **best** way to find a job. The best way is the way that works for you.

Look again at the Career Decision-Making Model on page 86. You have already considered the first five steps. The sixth step is to *put together a plan.*

Your ultimate goal is to find a job. Many methods are available that can help you find a job. Your success depends on how much time and energy you are willing to invest in your search. Keep in mind that there is no **best** way to find a job. The best way is the way that works for you.

You have decided on a career you want to pursue. Now it is time to do something about it. You want to do more than just dreaming about having a job. You want to put together a plan that will help make your dreams a reality.

On the following worksheet:

- Identify your career goal.
- List the steps you will take to accomplish your goal.
- Give yourself a deadline for each step. Decide what you need to do today, tomorrow, and next week.
- Make your deadlines reasonable.
- Sign your plan and date it.
- Share your completed worksheet with someone who is supportive and encouraging. Ask this person to sign and date the worksheet. Also, ask the person to check with you occasionally to be sure you are making progress.

Use another sheet of paper if you need more space.

My Plan of Action

My goal: _____

_____

_____

The steps I will take to reach this goal:

First step: _____ Deadline date: _____

Second step: _____ Deadline date: _____

Third step: _____ Deadline date: _____

Fourth step: _____ Deadline date: _____

Fifth step: _____ Deadline date: _____

_____ I understand that this is my plan and that I have a responsibility to myself to complete it and to review and update it regularly.

Signature _____ Date _____

I have shared this plan with _____

Signature _____ Date _____

WHAT'S NEXT?

In this chapter, you looked at the first six steps involved in making career decisions. You started by deciding to decide. You learned how to gather information about yourself, explore what's out there, and evaluate options and consequences. You made a decision about one career you want to pursue. You got information about putting together a plan.

In Chapter 7, you will look at another step in making career decisions. You will get information you will need if you decide to get additional education after high school.

Getting More Education After High School

You have considered careers that interest you. To get the career you want, you may need to get additional education or training after high school.

In this chapter, you will continue looking at the Career Decision-Making Model (page 86). The information here will help you answer these questions:

- Will additional education really benefit me?
- What jobs interest me? Do they require additional education?
- What are some training or education options?
- Which option is best for me?
- What if I do not have the money needed for additional schooling?

As you create your portfolio, you may want to include all or some of this chapter's worksheets. They can be valuable references for you.

Act

The seventh step in the Career Decision-Making Model (page 86) is to *act*. For you, acting may mean looking for a job. If so, you will get additional information in chapter 8.

For you, acting may mean you need to get additional training or education after high school. If so, this chapter will be especially helpful to you.

Maybe you plan to go on to college. You may be thinking of a two- or four-year degree. Or maybe you plan to get a master's, a Ph.D., or another professional degree.

Perhaps you're thinking of attending a trade or technical school. The military also offers training for many careers. Serving in the military is one way to earn scholarship money for a degree program.

Some businesses offer on-the-job training. In some careers, you can get your foot in the door by serving an apprenticeship.

Your choices may seem overwhelming. This chapter will help you make the right choice for you.

Does Education Pay Off?

You have looked at your interests, values, and skills. You have started exploring which careers fit your own individual mix. But there's something else to consider when choosing a career: How much money do you want to make?

You know that some jobs pay much better than others. One of the things you must decide is how much money you want to make. Base your decision on the kind of lifestyle you want. Everyone wants to earn a decent living. But people define *a decent living* differently.

> People with more education usually make more money than people with less education.

For some people, a decent living is one that provides enough money for the rent, the utilities, the groceries, and a few occasional extras. For other people, a decent living is one that provides enough money for a big house, a condo in a resort area, a sports car, vacations abroad, and a small army of servants.

You must decide for yourself what a decent living is. As you decide, consider this: Education and earnings are connected. In general, the more education you have, the more money you will make. Look at the following chart.

A person who has a **doctoral degree** will make about **$70,476** each year.

This is **$41,669 more** than what a person with a high school education will make.

A person who has a **master's degree** will make about **$55,302** each year.

This is **$26,495 more** than what a person with a high school education will make.

A person with a **bachelor's degree** will make about **$46,276** each year.

This is **$17,469 more** than what a person with a high school education will make.

A person with a **two-year/associate degree** will make about **$35,389** each year.

This is **$6,582 more** than what a person with a high school education will make.

Of course, these numbers are not correct 100% of the time. For example, you may know one person with a high school education and another person with a college degree. The high school graduate may make more than the college graduate. However, people with more education usually make more money than people with less education.

How Much Education Do You Need?

On pages 101–106 are the titles of the top jobs in the United States, as listed in the *Occupational Outlook Handbook*. These are the jobs that more than 87 percent of the population works in. The table also lists information about earnings and education. For detailed descriptions of any of the jobs listed, check your school library for the *Occupational Outlook Handbook* or the *Young Person's Occupational Outlook Handbook*.

How much money you make is only one thing that will make a job satisfying for you.

Look through the list of job titles in the first column of the following chart. Put a check mark by the jobs that interest you. Don't worry about whether you have the education you need to do the job. Just think about your skills, your interests, and how much money you need to make. Do these match the jobs you are interested in? If so, put a check mark beside the jobs. For now, don't eliminate a job just because you don't have enough education to be qualified.

Remember also that how much money you make is only one thing that will make a job satisfying for you. Other things may be more important to you than making lots of money. For example, if you had to choose between two jobs, you might choose the one that lets you help other people instead of the one that pays $50,000 per year. The kind of work you do may be more important to you than making money. The amount of money you make is important, but it does not guarantee success or happiness.

Look at the second column of the following chart. You will see a series of dollar signs ($). Here's how to interpret the information in that column:

$	=	$15,000 or less per year
$$	=	$15,001 to $23,000 per year
$$$	=	$23,001 to $28,000 per year
$$$$	=	$28,001 to $50,000 per year
$$$$$	=	$50,001 or more per year

Now look at the third column of the following chart. This information tells how much training and education you need for this kind of job. The information is abbreviated. Here's how to interpret the abbreviations:

Short-term OJT	=	On-the-job training that lasts up to six months
Long-term OJT	=	On-the-job training that lasts up to two or more years
Work experience	=	Work experience in a related job
Voc/tech training	=	Formal vocational or technical training received in a school, apprenticeship, cooperative-education program, or the military. This training can last from a few months to two or more years. It may combine classroom training with on-the-job experience.
Associate degree	=	A two-year college degree
Bachelor's degree	=	A four-year college degree
Master's degree	=	A bachelor's degree plus one or more years of additional education
Doctoral degree	=	A master's degree plus two or more years of additional education
Professional degree	=	A bachelor's degree plus two or more years of specialized education
Plus sign	=	The plus sign indicates that you need work experience in a related job as well as formal education. For example, "Bachelor's degree +" means you need a bachelor's degree plus work experience in a related job.

Top Jobs in the United States

Job Title	Earnings	Education & Training
Management and Business and Financial Operations Occupations		
_____ Accountants & Auditors	$$$$	Bachelor's degree
_____ Administrative Services Managers	$$$$	Work experience
_____ Advertising, Marketing, Promotions, Public Relations & Sales Managers	$$$$–$$$$$	Bachelor's degree +
_____ Budget Analysts	$$$$	Bachelor's degree
_____ Claims Adjusters, Appraisers, Examiners & Investigators	$$$–$$$$	Moderate OJT
_____ Computer & Information Systems Managers	$$$$$	Bachelor's degree
_____ Construction Managers	$$$$–$$$$$	Bachelor's degree
_____ Cost Estimators	$$$$	Associate degree to bachelor's degree +
_____ Education Administrators	$$$$–$$$$$	Master's degree
_____ Engineering & Natural Sciences Managers	$$$$$	Bachelor's degree +
_____ Farmers, Ranchers & Agricultural Managers	$$–$$$	Long-term OJT to bachelor's degree +
_____ Financial Analysts & Personal Financial Advisors	$$$$$	Bachelor's degree
_____ Financial Managers	$$$$$	Bachelor's degree +
_____ Food Service Managers	$$$$	Voc/tech training
_____ Funeral Directors	$$$$	Voc/tech training
_____ Human Resources, Training & Labor Relations Managers & Specialists	$$$$$	Master's degree
_____ Industrial Production Managers	$$$$–$$$$$	Bachelor's degree
_____ Insurance Underwriters	$$$$	Bachelor's degree
_____ Loan Counselors & Officers	$$$$	Bachelor's degree
_____ Lodging Managers	$$$–$$$$	Associate degree
_____ Management Analysts	$$$$–$$$$$	Bachelor's degree +
_____ Medical & Health Services Managers	$$$$$	Bachelor's degree +
_____ Property, Real Estate & Community Association Managers	$$$$	Bachelor's degree
_____ Purchasing Managers, Buyers & Purchasing Agents	$$$$$	Bachelor's degree
_____ Tax Examiners, Collectors & Revenue Agents	$$$$	Bachelor's degree
_____ Top Executives	$$$$–$$$$$	Bachelor's degree +
Professional and Related Occupations		
_____ Actors, Producers & Directors	$$$–$$$$$	Long-term OJT to bachelor's degree +
_____ Actuaries	$$$$–$$$$$	Bachelor's degree
_____ Aerospace Engineers	$$$$$	Bachelor's degree
_____ Agricultural & Food Scientists	$$$$	Bachelor's degree
_____ Agricultural Engineers	$$$$$	Bachelor's degree
_____ Announcers	$$$–$$$$	Voc/tech training to bachelor's degree +
_____ Architects, Except Landscape & Naval	$$$$–$$$$$	Bachelor's degree
_____ Archivists, Curators & Museum Technicians	$$$$	Master's degree
_____ Artists & Related Workers	$$$$$	Voc/tech training
_____ Athletes, Coaches, Umpires & Related Workers	$$–$$$$	Long-term OJT to bachelor's degree +
_____ Atmospheric Scientists	$$$$–$$$$$	Bachelor's degree
_____ Biological & Medical Scientists	$$$$–$$$$$	Doctoral degree
_____ Biomedical Engineers	$$$$$	Professional degree
_____ Broadcast & Sound Engineering Technicians & Radio Operators	$$$–$$$$	Bachelor's degree
_____ Cardiovascular Technologists & Technicians	$$$$	Associate degree
_____ Chemical Engineers	$$$$–$$$$$	Bachelor's degree
_____ Chemists & Materials Scientists	$$$$$	Bachelor's degree
_____ Chiropractors	$$$$$	Bachelor's degree
_____ Civil Engineers	$$$$–$$$$$	Bachelor's degree
_____ Clergy	$$$–$$$$	Professional degree

continues

continued

Job Title	Earnings	Education & Training
_____ Clinical Laboratory Technologists & Technicians	$$$$	Voc/tech training to bachelor's degree
_____ Computer Hardware Engineers	$$$$$	Bachelor's degree
_____ Computer Programmers	$$$$$	Voc/tech training to bachelor's degree
_____ Computer Software Engineers	$$$$–$$$$$	Bachelor's degree
_____ Computer Support Specialists & Systems Administrators	$$$$–$$$$$	Associate to bachelor's degree
_____ Conservation Scientists & Foresters	$$$$	Bachelor's degree
_____ Counselors	$$$$	Master's degree
_____ Court Reporters	$$$$	Voc/tech training
_____ Dancers & Choreographers	$$	Voc/tech training
_____ Dental Hygienists	$$$$$	Associate degree
_____ Dentists	$$$$$	Professional degree
_____ Designers	$$$$	Bachelor's degree
_____ Diagnostic Medical Sonographers	$$$$	Bachelor's degree
_____ Dietitians & Nutritionists	$$$$	Bachelor's degree
_____ Drafters	$$$–$$$$	Voc/tech training
_____ Economists & Market & Survey Researchers	$$$$–$$$$$	Bachelor's degree
_____ Electrical & Electronics Engineers, Except Computer	$$$$–$$$$$	Bachelor's degree
_____ Emergency Medical Technicians & Paramedics	$$	Voc/tech training
_____ Engineering Technicians	$$$$	Associate degree
_____ Engineers	$$$$$	Bachelor's degree
_____ Environmental Engineers	$$$$$	Bachelor's degree
_____ Environmental Scientists & Geoscientists	$$$$–$$$$$	Bachelor's degree
_____ Industrial Engineers, Including Health & Safety	$$$$–$$$$$	Bachelor's degree
_____ Instructional Coordinators	$$$$	Bachelor's to master's degree
_____ Judges, Magistrates & Other Judicial Workers	$$$$–$$$$$	Professional degree
_____ Landscape Architects	$$$$	Bachelor's degree
_____ Lawyers	$$$$–$$$$$	Professional degree
_____ Librarians	$$$$	Master's degree
_____ Library Technicians	$$$	Short-term OJT
_____ Licensed Practical & Licensed Vocational Nurses	$$$$	Bachelor's degree
_____ Materials Engineers	$$$$–$$$$$	Bachelor's degree
_____ Mathematicians	$$$$–$$$$$	Doctoral degree
_____ Mechanical Engineers	$$$$–$$$$$	Voc/tech training
_____ Medical Records & Health Information Technicians	$$	Associate degree
_____ Mining & Geological Engineers, Including Mining Safety Engineers	$$$$–$$$$$	Bachelor's degree
_____ Musicians, Singers & Related Workers	$$$–$$$$	Long-term OJT to bachelor's degree +
_____ News Analysts, Reporters & Correspondents	$$$–$$$$	Bachelor's degree
_____ Nuclear Engineers	$$$$$	Bachelor's degree
_____ Nuclear Medicine Technologists	$$$$	Associate degree
_____ Occupational Health & Safety Specialists & Technicians	$$$$	Bachelor's degree +
_____ Occupational Therapists	$$$$	Bachelor's degree +
_____ Operations Research Analysts	$$$$–$$$$$	Master's degree
_____ Opticians, Dispensing	$$$	Long-term OJT to voc/tech training
_____ Optometrists	$$$$$	Professional degree
_____ Paralegals & Legal Assistants	$$$$$	Associate degree
_____ Petroleum Engineers	$$$$$	Bachelor's degree
_____ Pharmacists	$$$$$	Bachelor's degree
_____ Pharmacy Technicians	$$	Work experience
_____ Photographers	$$	Bachelor's degree
_____ Physical Therapists	$$$$–$$$$$	Bachelor's degree
_____ Physician Assistants	$$$$$	Bachelor's degree
_____ Physicians & Surgeons	$$$$$	Professional degree
_____ Physicists & Astronomers	$$$$	Doctoral degree

© JIST Works

Job Title	Earnings	Education & Training
_____ Podiatrists	$$$$$	Professional degree
_____ Probation Officers & Correctional Treatment Specialists	$$$$	Bachelor's degree
_____ Protestant Ministers	$$$–$$$$	Professional degree
_____ Psychologists	$$$$–$$$$$	Master's degree to doctoral degree
_____ Public Relations Specialists	$$$$	Bachelor's degree
_____ Rabbis	$$$–$$$$	Professional degree
_____ Radiologic Technologists & Technicians	$$$$	Associate degree
_____ Recreational Therapists	$$$–$$$$	Bachelor's degree
_____ Registered Nurses	$$$$	Associate degree to bachelor's degree
_____ Respiratory Therapists	$$$$	Associate degree
_____ Roman Catholic Priests	$	Professional degree
_____ Science Technicians	$$$$–$$$$$	Associate degree
_____ Social & Human Service Assistants	$$	Moderate OJT
_____ Social Scientists, Other	$$$$	Master's degree
_____ Social Workers	$$$–$$$$	Bachelor's degree to master's degree
_____ Speech-Language Pathologists & Audiologists	$$$$	Master's degree
_____ Statisticians	$$$$–$$$$$	Bachelor's degree
_____ Surgical Technologists	$$$–$$$$	Voc/tech training
_____ Surveyors, Cartographers, Photogrammetrists & Surveying Technicians	$$$$	Voc/tech training + to bachelor's degree
_____ Systems Analysts, Computer Scientists & Database Administrators	$$$$$	Bachelor's degree
_____ Teacher Assistants	$$	Short-term OJT
_____ Teachers—Adult Literacy & Remedial & Self-Enrichment Education	$$$–$$$$	Work experience
_____ Teachers—Postsecondary	$$$$–$$$$$	Doctoral degree
_____ Teachers—Preschool, Kindergarten, Elementary, Middle & Secondary	$$$$	Bachelor's degree to master's degree
_____ Teachers—Special Education	$$$$	Bachelor's degree
_____ Television, Video & Motion Picture Camera Operators & Editors	$$$	Voc/tech training
_____ Urban & Regional Planners	$$$$	Master's degree
_____ Veterinarians	$$$$–$$$$$	Professional degree
_____ Writers & Editors	$$$$	Bachelor's degree

Service Occupations

Job Title	Earnings	Education & Training
_____ Animal Care & Service Workers	$$	Moderate OJT
_____ Barbers, Cosmetologists & Other Personal Appearance Workers	$$–$$$	Voc/tech training
_____ Building Cleaning Workers	$$–$$$$	Short-term OJT
_____ Chefs, Cooks & Food Preparation Workers	$$$	Moderate OJT
_____ Childcare Workers	$–$$$	Moderate OJT
_____ Correctional Officers	$$$–$$$$	Long-term OJT
_____ Dental Assistants	$$–$$$	Long-term OJT to work experience
_____ Firefighting Occupations	$$$–$$$$	Work experience
_____ Flight Attendants	$$$$	Long-term OJT to voc/tech training
_____ Food & Beverage Serving & Related Workers	$–$$	Short-term OJT
_____ Gaming Services Workers	$$–$$$	Short-term OJT
_____ Grounds Maintenance Workers	$$–$$$	Moderate OJT
_____ Medical Assistants	$$$	Long-term OJT to voc/tech training
_____ Medical Transcriptionists	$$$	Voc/tech training to associate degree
_____ Nursing, Psychiatric & Home Health Aides	$$	Short-term OJT
_____ Occupational Therapist Assistants & Aides	$$$–$$$$	Associate degree
_____ Personal & Home Care Aides	$–$$	Short-term OJT
_____ Pest Control Workers	$$	Moderate OJT

continues

continued

Job Title	Earnings	Education & Training
_____ Pharmacy Aides	$$	Moderate OJT
_____ Physical Therapist Assistants & Aides	$$–$$$$	Associate degree
_____ Police & Detectives	$$$–$$$$	Work experience
_____ Private Detectives & Investigators	$$$	Long-term OJT
_____ Recreation & Fitness Workers	$$	Voc/tech training
_____ Security Guards & Gaming Surveillance Officers	$$	Moderate OJT
Sales and Related Occupations		
_____ Cashiers	$–$$	Short-term OJT
_____ Counter & Rental Clerks	$–$$	Short-term OJT
_____ Demonstrators, Product Promoters & Models	$$–$$$$$	Short-term OJT
_____ Insurance Sales Agents	$$$$	Bachelor's degree
_____ Real Estate Brokers & Sales Agents	$$$	Work experience
_____ Retail Salespersons	$–$$$	Short-term OJT
_____ Sales Engineers	$$$$$	Bachelor's degree
_____ Sales Representatives—Wholesale & Manufacturing	$$$–$$$$$	Bachelor's degree
_____ Sales Worker Supervisors	$$–$$$$	Associate degree
_____ Securities, Commodities & Financial Services Sales Agents	$$$$$	Bachelor's degree
_____ Travel Agents	$$–$$$	Voc/tech training
Office and Administrative Support Occupations		
_____ Bill & Account Collectors	$$$	Long-term OJT to associate degree
_____ Billing & Posting Clerks & Machine Operators	$$–$$$	Short-term OJT
_____ Bookkeeping, Accounting & Auditing Clerks	$$–$$$	Moderate OJT to voc/tech training
_____ Brokerage Clerks	$$$$	Bachelor's degree
_____ Cargo & Freight Agents	$$$$	Short-term OJT
_____ Communications Equipment Operators	$$	Short-term OJT
_____ Computer Operators	$$$	Voc/tech training
_____ Couriers & Messengers	$$	Short-term OJT
_____ Credit Authorizers, Checkers & Clerks	$$$	Short- to long-term OJT
_____ Customer Service Representatives	$$$	Short-term OJT
_____ Data Entry & Information Processing Workers	$$–$$$	Voc/tech training
_____ Desktop Publishers	$$$$	Voc/tech training to bachelor's degree
_____ Dispatchers	$$$$	Moderate OJT
_____ File Clerks	$$	Short-term OJT
_____ Financial Clerks	$$	High school diploma to associate degree
_____ Gaming Cage Workers	$$	High school diploma
_____ Hotel, Motel & Resort Desk Clerks	$–$$	Short- to long-term OJT
_____ Human Resources Assistants, Except Payroll & Timekeeping	$$$$	Short-term OJT
_____ Information & Record Clerks	$–$$	Short- to long-term OJT
_____ Interviewers	$$	Moderate OJT
_____ Library Assistants, Clerical	$$	Short-term OJT
_____ Material Recording, Scheduling, Dispatching & Distributing Occupations, Except Postal Workers	$$–$$$	Moderate OJT
_____ Meter Readers, Utilities	$$$	Short-term OJT
_____ Office & Administrative Support Worker Supervisors & Managers	$$$$	Work experience
_____ Office Clerks, General	$$	Short-term OJT
_____ Order Clerks	$$$	Short-term OJT
_____ Payroll & Timekeeping Clerks	$$–$$$	Short-term OJT
_____ Postal Service Workers	$$$$	Short-term OJT
_____ Procurement Clerks	$$–$$$	Associate degree
_____ Production, Planning & Expediting Clerks	$$$$	Long-term OJT
_____ Receptionists & Information Clerks	$$	Short-term OJT
_____ Reservation & Transportation Ticket Agents & Travel Clerks	$$$	Short-term OJT

Job Title	Earnings	Education & Training
_____ Secretaries & Administrative Assistants	$$$$	Short-term OJT to voc/tech training to bachelor's degree
_____ Shipping, Receiving & Traffic Clerks	$$	Short-term OJT
_____ Stock Clerks & Order Fillers	$$	Short-term OJT
_____ Tellers	$$	Short-term OJT
_____ Weighers, Measurers, Checkers & Samplers, Recordkeeping	$$$	Short-term OJT

Farming, Fishing, and Forestry Occupations

Job Title	Earnings	Education & Training
_____ Agricultural Workers	$$	Short-term OJT to bachelor's degree
_____ Fishers & Fishing Vessel Operators	$$–$$$$	Long-term OJT to voc-tech training
_____ Forest, Conservation & Logging Workers	$$$	Short-term OJT

Construction Trades and Related Workers

Job Title	Earnings	Education & Training
_____ Boilermakers	$$$$	Long-term OJT
_____ Brickmasons, Blockmasons & Stonemasons	$$$$	Voc-tech training
_____ Carpenters	$$$$	Long-term OJT
_____ Carpet, Floor & Tile Installers & Finishers	$$$–$$$$	Moderate OJT
_____ Cement Masons, Concrete Finishers, Segmental Pavers & Terrazzo Workers	$$$–$$$$	Long-term OJT
_____ Construction & Building Inspectors	$$$–$$$$	Work experience
_____ Construction Equipment Operators	$$$–$$$$	Voc-tech training
_____ Construction Laborers	$$$–$$$$	Long-term OJT
_____ Drywall Installers, Ceiling Tile Installers & Tapers	$$$–$$$$	Moderate OJT
_____ Electricians	$$$$	Long-term OJT to voc/tech training
_____ Elevator Installers & Repairers	$$$$	Long-term OJT
_____ Glaziers	$$$–$$$$	Long-term OJT
_____ Hazardous Materials Removal Workers	$$$	Work experience
_____ Insulation Workers	$$$–$$$$	Moderate OJT
_____ Painters & Paperhangers	$$$	Short-term OJT
_____ Pipelayers, Plumbers, Pipefitters & Steamfitters	$$$$	Long-term OJT to voc/tech training
_____ Plasterers & Stucco Masons	$$$–$$$$	Long-term OJT
_____ Roofers	$$$$	Moderate OJT
_____ Sheet Metal Workers	$$$–$$$$	Short- to long-term OJT
_____ Structural & Reinforcing Iron & Metal Workers	$$$$	Long-term OJT

Installation, Maintenance, and Repair Occupations

Job Title	Earnings	Education & Training
_____ Aircraft & Avionics Equipment Mechanics & Service Technicians	$$$$	Voc/tech training
_____ Automotive Body & Related Repairers	$$$$	Long-term OJT to voc/tech training
_____ Automotive Service Technicians & Mechanics	$$$$	Long-term OJT to voc/tech training
_____ Coin, Vending & Amusement Machine Servicers & Repairers	$$$	Long-term OJT
_____ Computer, Automated Teller & Office Machine Repairers	$$$$	Long-term OJT to voc/tech training
_____ Diesel Service Technicians & Mechanics	$$$$	Long-term OJT to voc/tech training
_____ Electrical & Electronics Installers & Repairers	$$$–$$$$	Voc/tech training
_____ Electronic Home Entertainment Equipment Installers & Repairers	$$$	Long-term OJT to voc/tech training
_____ Heating, Air-Conditioning & Refrigeration Mechanics & Installers	$$$$	Long-term OJT to voc/tech training
_____ Heavy Vehicle & Mobile Equipment Service Technicians & Mechanics	$$$–$$$$	Long-term OJT to voc/tech training

continues

continues

Job Title	Earnings	Education & Training
_____ Home Appliance Repairers	$$$$	Long-term OJT
_____ Industrial Machinery Installation, Repair & Maintenance Workers	$$$$	Long-term OJT
_____ Line Installers & Repairers	$$$–$$$$	Long-term OJT
_____ Precision Instrument & Equipment Repairers	$$$$	High school diploma to voc/tech training
_____ Radio & Telecommunications Equipment Installers & Repairers	$$$–$$$$	Voc/tech training
_____ Small-Engine Mechanics	$$–$$$	Long-term OJT to voc/tech training

Production Occupations

Job Title	Earnings	Education & Training
_____ Assemblers & Fabricators	$$$–$$$$	Long-term OJT
_____ Bookbinders & Bindery Workers	$$$	Long-term OJT
_____ Computer-Control Programmers & Operators	$$$$	Long-term OJT to voc/tech training
_____ Dental Laboratory Technicians	$$$–$$$$	Long-term OJT
_____ Food Processing Occupations	$$	Short-term OJT
_____ Inspectors, Testers, Sorters, Samplers & Weighers	$$$	Work experience to long-term OJT
_____ Jewelers & Precious Stone & Metal Workers	$$$	Long-term OJT
_____ Machine Setters, Operators & Tenders— Metal & Plastic	$$$$	Short-term OJT to voc/tech training
_____ Machinists	$$$$	Long-term OJT to voc/tech training
_____ Metal Workers & Plastic Workers	$$–$$$	Short- to long-term OJT
_____ Ophthalmic Laboratory Technicians	$$	Long-term OJT
_____ Painting & Coating Workers, Except Construction & Maintenance	$$	Long-term OJT
_____ Photographic Process Workers & Processing Machine Operators	$$–$$$	Long-term OJT
_____ Power Plant Operators, Distributors & Dispatchers	$$$$	Long-term OJT
_____ Prepress Technicians & Workers	$$$	Long-term OJT to voc/tech training
_____ Printing Machine Operators	$$$	Voc/tech training
_____ Semiconductor Processors	$$$	Associate degree
_____ Stationary Engineers & Boiler Operators	$$$$	Long-term OJT
_____ Textile, Apparel & Furnishings Occupations	$$	Long-term OJT
_____ Tool & Die Makers	$$$$	Long-term OJT to voc/tech training
_____ Water & Liquid Waste Treatment Plant & System Operators	$$$–$$$$	Long-term OJT
_____ Welding, Soldering & Brazing Workers	$$$	Long-term OJT to voc/tech training
_____ Woodworkers	$$	Long-term OJT

Transportation and Material Moving Occupations

Job Title	Earnings	Education & Training
_____ Air Traffic Controllers	$$$$$	Long-term OJT
_____ Aircraft Pilots & Flight Engineers	$$$$$	Bachelor's degree
_____ Bus Drivers	$$$	Moderate OJT
_____ Material Moving Occupations	$$$–$$$$	Moderate OJT
_____ Rail Transportation Occupations	$$$–$$$$	Work experience to long-term OJT
_____ Taxi Drivers & Chauffeurs	$$	Short-term OJT
_____ Truck Drivers & Driver/Sales Workers	$$–$$$	Short-term OJT
_____ Water Transportation Occupations	$$$–$$$$	Voc/tech training

Job Opportunities in the Armed Forces

Job Title	Earnings	Education & Training
_____ Job Opportunities in the Armed Forces	$$$	Long-term OJT

Go to the Experts

Do you know of someone who does the kind of work you want to do? If not, ask your parents, your teachers, your counselor, and your friends if they know anyone who does that kind of work. When you get the name of someone, call and ask the person if he or she will meet with you in person or talk to you about the job on the phone. Most people love to talk about themselves and their work.

You can also search the Internet for information. Look at job postings to see what kind of qualifications a person needs for the job.

Another idea is to call a person who supervises people in the job you like. This gives you an idea about what managers look for in the people they hire. Ask the questions on the following worksheet. Record your answers. If you plan to make more than one call, make copies of this page first. Then you will have a form to use with each call.

I Talk to the Experts

How much education do I need to do this job? _____

_____

What kind of training do I need to do this job? _____

_____

If I need college, is there a specific major I should pursue? _____

_____

Do I need specialized training?_____

_____

Is training provided on the job, or will I have to complete a training program before I can be hired? _____

_____

Where did you [the expert] receive your training? _____

_____

What schools or technical institutes are known for training people in this kind of work?

_____

Are there any professional associations or unions I can contact for more information?

_____

On-the-Job Training

You could go straight from high school to work and let your employer train you to do your job. On-the-job training is generally offered to new employees who do not yet have the skills to do a job. It may also be offered to experienced employees who are learning new skills needed for job advancement.

> On-the-job training is generally offered to new employees who do not yet have the skills to do a job.

On-the-job training may involve classroom instruction or hands-on activity or both. Some companies will even pay you while you train. In other companies, you may have to go through a training program first and then take a test to qualify for a paid position.

Review the following chart for some of the advantages and disadvantages to on-the-job training.

Advantages	Disadvantages
You begin earning money immediately.	You will probably just learn how to do one job, so you may have a hard time moving to a different job.
You do not have to go into debt to get the training.	You will probably make less money than you would if you got additional schooling after high school.
You develop skills for a specialized job.	

Look at the jobs list on pages 101–106 to find jobs that require only on-the-job training.

To find out about on-the-job training opportunities, contact companies and organizations in your area. Ask if they provide training programs. Use the following worksheet as a guide in getting information. When you talk to a company about on-the-job training, be sure you get answers to the questions in the worksheet.

I Consider On-the-Job Training

Am I guaranteed a job after I complete my on-the-job training? _____

_____

What will my training qualify me to do? _____

_____

Will I receive some kind of certification after I complete the training? _____

_____

Will there be opportunities for more training later? _____

_____

What courses should I be taking in high school to prepare for the job? _____

_____

_____

Apprenticeships

Apprenticeships are similar to on-the-job training programs. They can last from one to six years. Apprenticeships include some classroom instruction.

Different occupations have different apprentice-ship standards and requirements. Apprentices usu-ally work about 1,000 hours in each six-month period. Apprentices usually receive a total of 2,000 to 12,000 hours of training.

> Many employers prefer to hire people who received training in a registered apprenticeship program.

Formal testing may be required for an employee to be recognized as qualified. Apprenticeship Completion Certificates are available through the U.S. Department of Labor, Employment and Training Administration.

You can find apprenticeship information by searching the Internet with the keyword *apprenticeship* or by visiting the Department of Labor's Web site at www.doleta.gov.

Apprentices must have a high school diploma or a General Education Development Test Certificate (GED). Apprentices must be physically able to perform the work of the trade. Apprentices must be at least 16 years old. Most apprentices are at least 18 years old.

Completing an apprenticeship is a good way to get into certain jobs. Many employers prefer to hire people who received training in a registered apprentice-ship program.

People who were apprentices tend to be better workers than people who receive only informal training. Also, they are more likely to become supervisors than are people who had only informal training. Even if you are unskilled, an apprenticeship can help you get your qualifications in a chosen trade.

Review the following chart for some of the advantages and disadvantages of apprenticeships.

Advantages	Disadvantages
You can work while you learn.	You will probably have to be an apprentice for several years.
You will work under the close supervision of a skilled worker.	You will probably be paid about half as much as an experienced worker is paid.
You will learn all aspects of a job.	You may not be able to find an apprenticeship in your area of interest.

According to the most recent information from the Department of Labor, the top occupations open to apprentices are

- Cook
- Painter
- Machinist
- Millwright
- Electrician
- Boilermaker
- Operating Engineer
- Correction Officer
- Power Plant Operator
- Electronics Mechanic
- Construction Craft Laborer

- Roofer
- Plumber
- Carpenter
- Bricklayer
- Pipe Fitter
- Fire Fighter
- Sheet Metal Worker
- Tool and Die Maker
- Maintenance Mechanic
- Structural-Steel Worker
- Telecommunication Technician

Be sure to ask a lot of questions before accepting an apprenticeship. The following worksheet can serve as a guide.

I Consider Finding an Apprenticeship

Questions I want to ask:

How long will my apprenticeship last? _____

_____

Will I work full time during the apprenticeship? _____

_____

How much money will I receive during my apprenticeship? _____

_____

How much time will I spend in the classroom? _____

_____

How much time will I spend on the job? _____

_____

What tools will I need? _____

_____

Do I have to supply my own tools? _____

_____

What are my chances of getting a related job at the end of the apprenticeship? _____

_____

Will I be certified at the end of the apprenticeship? _____

_____

Trade or Technical School

For some occupations, trade schools are the way to go. A trade or technical school allows you to take extensive coursework in the field you are studying. Technical institutes often employ industry professionals to teach their courses.

These programs provide an excellent way for employees to learn job skills. Classes are generally available beginning at a high-school level. Only a few schools provide general education courses. Most focus on skills related to a particular job. These schools offer certificates of achievement or two-year degrees.

> Trade and technical schools offer a direct route to certain careers.

Trade and technical schools offer a direct route to certain careers. You must do your homework to find the best school for you.

Review the following chart for some of the advantages and disadvantages of trade or technical schools.

Advantages	Disadvantages
You can complete the program in about two years.	You may have to spend a lot to attend a technical school. You may even pay more than you would if you went to a community college.
You will learn from people already working in the field.	You may be expected to take a full load each semester, so you would not be able to work full time.
You will have valuable career services available through the school.	You may find that trade schools are not regulated well. This means that quality varies greatly from one school to another.
You focus on just one career, so you get into the workforce sooner.	

© JIST Works

Check the jobs list on pages 101–106 to see what careers require technical or trade school education. Be sure to investigate schools carefully. Be sure the school you choose is accredited under the standards of the occupation you choose. Contact your local Chamber of Commerce or Better Business Bureau for additional information.

Use the following worksheet as a guide when you research a school. Be sure to get each of these questions answered before you sign an agreement.

I Investigate Trade or Technical Schools

Questions I want to ask:

What is the accrediting organization for schools that offer programs for people in my career?_____

_____

Is this school accredited by that organization?_____

_____

Is financial aid available to students? _____

_____

What is the current cost of tuition?_____

_____

How much does the cost of tuition increase each year? _____

_____

What percentage of students find related work after completing this program? _____

_____

Does the school offer job search services?_____

_____

Can the school provide a list of companies where graduates are working? _____

_____

Associate Degree

An associate degree can be earned at a community or junior college or from a traditional four-year college. Associate degrees usually require two years of full-time study. They are usually connected directly to an occupation.

Sometimes people complete a two-year associate degree and then decide they want to get a four-year bachelor's degree. That's okay. The time isn't wasted. The credits the person earned in the associate degree program can usually can be applied toward a bachelor's degree.

> Just two more years of school after high school can make a big difference in how much money a person earns.

Look at the chart on page 99 to see how much more a person with an associate degree makes than a person with a high school degree. Just two more years of school after high school can make a big difference in how much money a person earns.

Review the following chart for one of the advantages and one of the disadvantages of getting an associate degree.

Advantages	Disadvantages
You can earn an associate degree at a community college.	You may apply for a job that someone with a bachelor's degree also applies for. In areas other than education, you and the other person may be equally qualified. If so, the employer will probably hire the person with the bachelor's degree.
Your tuition and living expenses will be much less than they would be at a traditional college.	

Check the jobs list on pages 101–106 to see what careers require associate degrees.

For more information about associate degrees, contact community colleges in your area. Also contact traditional colleges or universities to see what associate degrees they offer. Be sure to ask the questions in the following worksheet.

I Think About Getting an Associate Degree

Questions I want to ask:

Is the school accredited?_____

_____

Is financial aid available? _____

_____

What is the current cost of tuition?_____

_____

How much does tuition increase from year to year? _____

_____

How long will it take me to earn my associate degree? _____

_____

Will the associate degree I'm considering apply toward a bachelor's degree if I decide to continue my education? _____

_____

Does the school offer job-search assistance?_____

_____

What percentage of students find related work after completing this program? _____

_____

Bachelor's Degree

When people talk about a college education, they usually think of a bachelor's degree. These degrees usually require four years of full-time study. Bachelor's degrees can be earned at a college or university.

In the first two years of a traditional four-year college program, you will study a variety of subjects. These include English, math, sociology, history, and a foreign language. In the final two years, you will specialize in one subject area. This subject area is called your major. Your degree will indicate your major. For example, you might get a Bachelor of Arts (B.A.) in English or a Bachelor of Science (B.S.) in Psychology.

There are now more ways than ever to finance an education.

Review the following chart if you are considering a bachelor's degree.

Advantages	Disadvantages
Your degree will be valued by employers.	Your education will be costly.
Employers will see you as a person who has a broad base of knowledge, who can stick with a program, and who knows how to learn.	You will be in school for about 4 years.

Even though a four-year degree is expensive, you can earn the money back in your salary difference within a few years. The good news is that there are now more ways than ever to finance an education. Check with the colleges that interest you. They can give you information about costs and about financial aid.

Look at the jobs list on pages 101–106 to get an idea of the kinds of jobs that require a four-year bachelor's degree.

For more information, check with your school counselors and teachers. Look in your school or public library for a college guide. These books compare colleges' costs, student life, academic standards, and just about anything else you can think of.

As you consider colleges, be sure to ask a lot of questions. Use the following worksheet as a guide.

I Consider a Bachelor's Degree

Questions I want to ask about the college and my degree program:

Is the college accredited? _____

Who accredits the college? _____

_____

What percentage of students graduates within four years?_____

_____

Will I be required to live on campus? _____

Does the school offer job-search assistance?_____

_____

What is the total semester cost for tuition, books and supplies, and room and board?

_____

How much do those costs increase each year? _____

_____

What is the deadline for applying for admission? _____

_____

What is the deadline for applying for financial aid? _____

_____

What courses should I be taking in high school to prepare for college? ___

_____

Military Training

Thousands of young men and women join the military each year. The military provides a way for these people to get a good education and a good career. Some people decide to stay in the military and make it a career. Others do not.

> The military provides a way for people to get a good education and a good career.

The important thing is to make an informed decision. Talk with your local service recruiter. Ask questions. Take time to think about your choices. Talk with family and friends. Try to find people who have served in the military. Talk to with them about their experiences.

If you want to join the military, you will have to take the Armed Services Vocational Aptitude Battery (ASVAB). The military uses the ASVAB to identify which jobs in the military will match your skills and talents. Contact your school's career center or your local recruiter's office to get a copy of the ASVAB Information Pamphlet. This pamphlet tells you more about the test and gives you some sample questions.

Review the following chart if you are considering joining the military.

Advantages	Disadvantages
You can get training that will help you find a good job when your service ends.	You cannot change your mind and drop out after you sign on the dotted line. You are committed.
You will receive financial assistance to attend college when you complete your service.	You will give up a lot of control over your life while you are in the military. You will have to go wherever you are sent, even to dangerous territories in other countries.

Look at the jobs list on pages 101–106. Many of the jobs that require on-the-job training are jobs you could get with the training you receive in the military.

Before you sign up to join the military, ask your service recruiter the questions on the following worksheet.

I Consider Joining the Military

Questions I want to ask:

If I sign up, how long will I have to be in the military? _____

Do I have any say in where I will be stationed? _____

Where am I most likely to be stationed? _____

_____

What will be my base pay? _____

What jobs in the military do my ASVAB scores qualify me for? _____

_____

What are my chances of getting trained in the job I want? _____

_____

Are there any other tests I must pass in order to get the job I want? _____

_____

Checking Out Schools

Some people decide early in life where they will get their education or training. But most people consider several options. Take your time in making a decision about school. Talk with the admissions people in every school you are considering.

The following worksheet can serve as a guide. Fill in the information you receive about each school. You will need to make additional copies of the worksheet so you have one for each school.

I Check Out Schools

School: _____

City: _____ State: _____ ZIP: _____

Expenses per year: _____

Accredited by: _____

Program requirements: _____

_____

Notes about other information: _____

_____

Getting Financial Aid

You already know that the cost of an education can be huge. But consider this: You can almost certainly find the money you need for your education. Nearly half of all college, technical, and trade school students in the United States receive financial aid.

> All fifty states offer some kind of financial aid based on need. The federal government also offers student financial aid.

State Aid

All fifty states offer some kind of financial aid based on need. Many offer merit scholarships to students who stay in-state for college. Some offer loans to students. Call your state's department of higher education for information about your state's programs. You can also ask your teacher or school counselor.

Federal Aid

The federal government also offers student financial aid. Here is a brief look at some major federal programs offering financial aid. The financial aid counselor at the school you're considering can give you additional information. Be sure to ask what forms you need to fill out and what deadlines you need to be aware of.

Pell Grants

This money does not have to be repaid when you finish school. The grants are awarded based on financial need. They are available to students who are pursuing their first undergraduate degree.

Supplementary Education Opportunity Grants

This money does not have to be repaid. The grants are awarded to students with great financial need.

Perkins Loans

This is money that colleges loan to their students. These loans must be repaid when the student graduates or leaves school. They are based on financial need. The loans have a low, fixed interest rate. The student pays no interest while in school. The money comes from the government, but the school makes the decision about who gets the loans.

Stafford Loans

These are loans made by banks, credit unions, and savings and loan associations. The loans are guaranteed by the government. Your high school counselor or college admissions officer can tell you who to call for information. If you qualify for one of these loans, the government pays the interest on your loan while you are in school.

Direct Student Loans

This money is available through the U.S. Department of Education. Loans are processed through colleges and universities.

Work-Study Program

This program allows students to work at jobs at their school or at a nonprofit organization. The student's salary helps pay the cost of his or her education. The program is based on financial need.

Federal Government Determines Need

The federal government uses a standard formula to determine whether a person qualifies for financial assistance. Here's a summary of what you have to do to request aid: List the total cost for a year of school; include tuition, fees, books, supplies, housing, meals, transportation, and personal expenses. List your own income and savings; include money you make at your current or summer job. List your family's income, savings, and assets.

Think of it this way:

- Estimated cost of your education
- Estimated resources you already have
- Estimated need (the difference between how much your education will cost and how much money you have)

The following worksheet can help you prepare for a meeting with the financial aid counselor at the school you want to attend. Fill out the worksheet and take it with you to the meeting.

My Costs and Resources

Estimated cost of my education

Tuition and fees: _____

Books and supplies: _____

Housing: _____

Meals: _____

Transportation: _____

Personal expenses: _____

   Total estimated cost: _____

Estimated resources I already have

Income from my summer job: _____

Income from my job during the school year: _____

My savings: _____

My parents' income: _____

My parents' savings: _____

My parents' assets (including our home): _____

   Total estimated resources: _____

Schedule Your Success

On the following pages are four worksheets that will help keep you on track as you prepare for college or other training after high school.

My Junior Year Courses

The following courses will help prepare me for my chosen career.

First Semester

_____

_____

_____

_____

_____

_____

_____

Second Semester

_____

_____

_____

_____

_____

_____

_____

_____

My Junior Year Timeline

	Date Due	Done
Talk with my high school guidance counselor about career information.	_____	_____
Begin informational interviews with people employed in jobs that interest me.	_____	_____
Sign up for the PSAT test if I'm planning to continue my education.	_____	_____
Write to colleges, technical institutes, or trade schools for information and catalogs.	_____	_____
Join a job club or take a part-time job that will help prepare me for my chosen field.	_____	_____
Attend college or job fairs in my community.	_____	_____
Visit nearby colleges, technical institutes, or trade schools. Schedule advance meetings with admissions and financial aid officers.	_____	_____
Look through school catalogs for information about admissions tests and deadlines.	_____	_____
Take the ACT or SAT, as practice.	_____	_____
Inquire about accommodations for any physical or learning disabilities I have.	_____	_____

My Senior Year Courses

The following courses will help prepare me for my chosen career.

First Semester

_____

_____

_____

_____

_____

_____

_____

_____

Second Semester

_____

_____

_____

_____

_____

_____

_____

_____

My Senior Year Timeline

	Date Due	Done
Meet with my guidance counselor to make sure I am on schedule to graduate.	_____	_____
Sign up for any courses I must have to graduate.	_____	_____
Take the ACT or SAT.	_____	_____
Visit schools that interest me.	_____	_____
Attend job and college fairs.	_____	_____
Narrow my choices to five or six schools.	_____	_____
Write down deadlines for admissions and financial aid applications for those schools.	_____	_____
Meet with my school counselor to discuss my education choices and financial aid.	_____	_____
Arrange for teachers to write letters of recommendation. Ask for copies of the letters to keep in my portfolio.	_____	_____
Complete and mail all admissions forms by deadlines. Keep copies.	_____	_____
Complete and mail all financial aid applications by deadlines. Keep copies.	_____	_____

WHAT'S NEXT?

This chapter provided you with information about getting additional education or training after high school. You learned how to evaluate various programs. You considered some options for getting financial aid.

In Chapter 8, you will find information about getting and keeping a job. You will need this information if you plan to start working after high school. You will also need it if you plan to get additional education after high school.

Chapter 8

Getting and Keeping a Job

In this chapter, you will finish the decision-making process you started in Chapter 6 using the Career Decision-Making Model (page 86). You have identified some possible careers. You may have determined that you do not need additional schooling for the jobs that interest you.

Now you are ready to put together a plan for landing a job. You will also need to know how to keep your job.

This chapter will help answer these questions:

- What tools and information will I need in my job search?

- When I am offered a job, how can I decide if it's the right job for me?

- After I find a job, what can I do to help ensure that I keep my job?

- What should I do if I decide my plan is not working for me?

You are well on your way to finding the right job for you. When you complete this chapter, you will have the confidence and knowledge needed for finding and keeping a job. For your own reference, you may want to include some of the worksheets in this chapter in your portfolio.

Act

The seventh step in the Career Decision-Making Model (page 86) is to *act*. For you, acting may mean you need to get additional training or education after high school. If so, Chapter 7 gave you information on how to pursue that education and training.

> Your dreams can become a reality—but only if you take action to make it so.

For you, acting may mean looking for a job. If so, the information in this chapter will be especially helpful to you.

The actions you take will depend on the steps you listed on the "My Plan of Action" worksheet (page 96). Your dreams can become a reality—but only if you take action to make it so.

When you look for a job, you need certain tools. The following sections describe some of those tools.

Job Applications

You will fill out applications before interviews or during the hiring process. Often, your job application gives employers their first look at you. How you fill out a job application shows whether you can do the following:

> Your job application gives employers their first look at you.

1. **Prepare and think ahead.** When you fill out an application, take with you the things you need. Take a copy of the worksheet called "My Job Application Fact Sheet" on page 128. Take at least two pens and pencils. Also take a copy of your resume to submit with the application or to leave with the employer (more on resumes in the following section).

   Remember: The person who hands you the application will talk to the person who interviews you. If you don't come prepared, the interviewer is sure to find out.

2. **Follow instructions and use accurate information.** Every job requires you to follow written instructions, rules, or procedures. You will be expected to read and understand. Be sure you fill out the job application correctly.

   Read the entire application before you start to fill it out. Make sure you understand the instructions in each section. Follow the instructions exactly. If the application says to print, be sure you print. Leave blank any section that says, "For employer's use only" or "Do not write below this line."

   Some applications ask you to list your most recent job first; others want the list in the reverse order. Read carefully.

   Be honest. If you are hired for the job and your employer discovers that you have intentionally lied on the application, you will likely be terminated.

3. **Complete a document neatly and follow through on a task.** Crossed-out or poorly erased information gives a negative impression that reflects on the quality of your work. Don't leave any sections or lines blank. Avoid writing "see above" or "see resume." Fill out the information requested. If you don't, the employer may assume you will not follow through on the details of a job. Of course, some questions may not apply to you. For these questions, put "N/A" (not applicable) in the space.

Use the following worksheet to organize the information you need for filling out applications. Refer to the worksheets you completed in previous chapters. They have information you need for filling in the following worksheet.

My Job Application Fact Sheet

Identification

Name: _____

Street address: _____

City: _____ State: _____ ZIP: _____

Current phone number or a number where a message can be left: _____

E-mail address: _____

Social Security number: _____ Driver's license number: _____

Name and telephone number of a person to contact in an emergency: _____

_____

Type of job desired: _____

_____

_____

Name of position I am applying for: _____

Date available to begin work: _____ Salary or pay rate expected: _____

Previous Employment

Job title: _____

Employer: _____

Street address: _____

City: _____ State: _____ ZIP: _____

Phone: _____ Fax: _____

Dates employed: _____ Reason for leaving: _____

Special skills demonstrated: _____

_____

_____

Job title: _____

Employer: _____

Street address: _____

City: _____ State: _____ ZIP: _____

Phone: _____ Fax: _____

Dates employed: _____ Reason for leaving: _____

Special skills demonstrated: _____

_____

_____

Job title: _____

Employer: _____

Street address: _____

City: _____ State: _____ ZIP: _____

Phone: _____ Fax: _____

Dates employed: _____ Reason for leaving: _____

Special skills demonstrated: _____

_____

_____

Formal Education

School most recently attended: _____

Address: _____

Dates attended: _____ Degree earned: _____

Activities, honors, clubs, sports: _____

_____

School: _____

Address: _____

Dates attended: _____ Degree earned: _____

Activities, honors, clubs, sports: _____

_____

continues

continued

References

Name: _____

Street address: _____

City: _____ State: _____ ZIP: _____

Phone: _____

Relationship (employer, teacher, clergy): _____

Name: _____

Street address: _____

City: _____ State: _____ ZIP: _____

Phone: _____

Relationship (employer, teacher, clergy): _____

Name: _____

Street address: _____

City: _____ State: _____ ZIP: _____

Phone: _____

Relationship (employer, teacher, clergy): _____

Resumes

You have already done much of the work needed to put together your resume. Employers want more than a list of job duties or where you worked and when. They are interested in how well you did your job and what skills and experience you have to offer. They want to know your strengths and what you accomplished. Review the worksheets in previous chapters to identify information you want to include in your resume.

Also look through the other documents you have filed in your portfolio. Review your school records, training certificates, and letters of recommendation for information to put in your resume.

> Employers want more than a list of job duties or where you worked and when. They are interested in how well you did your job and what skills and experience you have to offer. They want to know your strengths and what you accomplished.

The goal of writing a resume is to include just enough information to get an interview with the employer. Save the detailed information for the interview. Think of a resume as an advertisement you use to get an interview. Your resume should be

- Free of spelling, punctuation, grammar, or keyboard errors
- Short, concise, and specific
- Appealing to the eye and printed on quality paper

It should

- Emphasize what you have done and how you can benefit the employer
- Highlight the skills and strengths you have that relate to your target job

There are many ways to put a resume together. Remember the following points:

1. **Put your name, address, and phone number at the top of the resume.**

2. **Focus on the requirements of the job.** Make your resume fit the job you are applying for. Arrange the information on the resume to highlight certain skills or qualities. You may need two or three versions of your resume if you are applying for different kinds of jobs. Use the same basic information in each version of your resume.

   This is easy to do if you use a computer word-processing program. If you do not have a computer at home, you can probably use one at school or at the library.

3. **Highlight your most important assets.** This is the information you want to be sure the employer reads. Place it near the top of your resume.

   The top half of the first page of your resume is referred to as the "prime space" of your resume. The information in this area is what the employer will read first. Choose what is most important for the job you are applying for. Place this information in the prime space on your resume.

   Use bold lettering or divide the sections of your resume with lines to make it easier to read. You also may want to use bold type or underline the highlights of your resume. Bold or underlined type allows a prospective employer to scan the page and immediately see important information.

Keep copies of your resume in your portfolio. You can refer to it in the future. Updating or rearranging an old resume is easier than starting over.

Use the following worksheet as a guide. It can help you assemble the essential elements of your resume. When you have all the information, you can use a computer to prepare your resume. Try various formats until your resume says what you want it to say and looks the way you want it to look. Refer to worksheets you completed in previous chapters.

My Resume Worksheet

Name: _____

Address: _____

Telephone: _____ E-mail: _____

Summary

Here's a description of who I am: _____
_____
_____

Here is what I know about the career I'm interested in: _____
_____
_____
_____

Here are some of my skills and attributes: _____
_____
_____
_____

Here's a statement of how I can benefit the company and the employer: _____
_____
_____

Here's the kind of position I want: _____
_____

Education and Training

My recent education and training: _____
_____
_____

How this education and training matches my job target: _____
_____
_____

Current or Most Recent Job

Job title: _____

Skills needed: _____

_____

What I achieved: _____

_____

Summary of my experience: _____

_____

_____

Highlights of Qualifications

_____

_____

_____

_____

Employment History

_____

_____

_____

_____

Additional Education and Training

_____

_____

_____

_____

Cover Letters

 Tip If your cover letter has even one error, the interviewer will probably notice it. And all the work you did on your resume will be wasted.

You will spend a lot of time and energy to be sure your resume is perfect. And you should. You might think your cover letter isn't important since you just send it with the resume. But your cover letter is important. If your cover letter has even one error, the interviewer will probably notice it. And all the work you did on your resume will be wasted.

Your cover letter

- Shows a link between you and someone the interviewer already knows
- Describes your interest in the job
- Indicates what you know about the organization
- Provides additional information not included in your resume
- Shows how your skills, background, and strengths match the job requirements
- Explains any special circumstances
- Indicates your interest in being interviewed

To be effective, your cover letter should

- Be free of spelling, punctuation, grammar, or keyboard errors
- Use a standard business letter format printed on quality paper
- Be addressed to a specific individual by name and title, if possible
- Use the same font and basic format of your resume

Keep your cover letter short. It should just be one page unless you have an unusual amount of information to convey. Make sure your cover letter is easy to read. Avoid long paragraphs. Use short lists. If you are unsure about proper spelling and grammar, refer to a dictionary. Ask someone who has good writing skills to proofread your cover letter.

Your cover letter introduces the employer to your resume. It draws attention to information you want to highlight. Address your cover letter to a specific person if at all possible. Use your network to get the names of people to contact.

The following sample cover letter can serve as a guide for you as you write your cover letter.

Sara N. Wrap

7 High Street
Haverhill, MA 01850
Telephone: 978-374-5555
E-mail: saranwrap@aol.com

January 1, XXXX
Mr. Robert L. Smith
Vice President, Lawrence Memorial Hospital
123 Market Street
Sellersburg, IN 11122

Dear Mr. Smith:

I am a high school senior with experience in writing and editing. As my resume indicates, I have worked on our high school newspaper for three years. I will graduate at the beginning of May. I am writing in regard to your job opening for a Marketing Communications Assistant.

I am sure you will agree that my experience makes me the ideal candidate to aid the Marketing Coordinator at Lawrence Memorial Hospital. The following chart demonstrates my qualifications.

Your Requirements	My Qualifications
Writing experience	Extensive experience researching and writing stories and editorials for my high school newspaper
Ability to serve in a support position	Three years' experience working under the direction of the supervising faculty and the student managing editor
Ability to edit written materials	Assumed role of final proofreader and editor of copy submitted by other students

As requested, I have enclosed my resume with further details of my qualifications and accomplishments. I look forward to meeting with you to discuss how I will fit into your organization. I am certain you will agree that I can add value to your professional staff and assist your Marketing Coordinator. I will call you early next week to see if we might set a mutually convenient time to get together.

Sincerely,

Sara N. Wrap

Follow the format of the example to compose your own, personalized cover letter in the following worksheet.

My Cover Letter Outline

(my name) _____

(street address) _____

(city, state, ZIP) _____

(phone number) _____ (e-mail)_____

(other contact information) _____

(date) _____

(employer's name) _____

(employer's job title, company name)_____

(street address) _____

(city, state, ZIP) _____

Dear (employer's title and last name) _____

(paragraph stating what I know about the company or industry and telling the name of a referral if I have one) _____

_____

_____

(general statement of what I know about the position and why I am well suited to the position) _____

_____

_____

(more-specific description of the skills, abilities, and strengths I bring to the position—a chart or paragraph) _____

_____

_____

(concluding paragraph that states when and how I will follow up, requests an interview, and says thank you) _____

_____

_____

Sincerely,

(my signature) _____

(my printed name) _____

Employer Contacts

Tip When you are on the telephone, make sure you stand up straight. The tone and sound of your voice will be better.

In Chapter 5, you completed a diagram of your network. Refer to Figure 2 on page 79. The diagram shows the names of people you can contact for career information. Those same people can provide employer contacts and information about job openings. If you ask your network for this kind of help, you can expand your network. Then you will have many sources of information.

You will find that most people will want to help you if you make it easy for them. Remember that by accepting help you are obligated to give help to others in your network when the time comes.

One great, inexpensive way of expanding your network is to let your fingers do the walking! Many people think that making telephone calls to employers is difficult. If you are one of those people, having a telephone script can help. A script should include the following information:

- A greeting
- Your name
- The name of the contact person who suggested that you call
- The purpose of your call
- Two or three things about you that will interest the employer
- A request for a face-to-face meeting

Even with a script, you may be uncomfortable calling a stranger about job openings. If so, start by making practice calls to people you know. This will prepare you for calling people you do not know.

Sometimes an employer wants to interview you on the phone. This is a good thing. Before you call, be sure you have a copy of your resume handy. This will help you remember what you want to say about yourself. If you call an employer who decides to interview you on the phone right then, send the employer your resume and a thank-you letter as a follow-up.

When you are on the telephone, make sure you stand up straight. Obviously the interviewer cannot see you. But if you stand up straight, the tone and sound of your voice will be better.

The following worksheet will help you develop a phone script. When you have completed this exercise, practice reading your script aloud. Keep refining it until the words feel natural.

Make your script short. You want to sell yourself without sounding like a telemarketer. That means you need to get across all your vital information in the first 30 seconds or so. Time yourself when you practice saying your script aloud.

To conclude the phone call, ask when you can come in for an interview. Do not ask **if** you can come in but **when** you can come in. Make it hard for the employer to turn you down. After all, your goal is to get an interview. Fill in the following worksheet to help organize your thoughts and create your personalized phone script.

> Do not ask **if** you can come in but **when** you can come in. Make it hard for the employer to turn you down.

My Telephone Script

Good morning. My name is _____

I'm calling at the suggestion of (name of referral) _____,
a business acquaintance of yours. He/she said you might know of an opening in your organization or in another organization for a person of my abilities.

I have more than _____ years of experience in (description of my skills, abilities, and strengths; information about how well I perform my tasks and responsibilities) _____

_____

_____

_____

_____

When would be a good time for me to come in for an interview?

Interviews

The more you prepare for an interview, the better you do. Two key steps to preparing for interviews are finding out about the employer and practicing the interview.

Finding Out About the Employer

Employers like applicants who take the time to get information about the job and the company. If you do this, the employer knows that you have selected the job and the company carefully. Information you gather about the company will help you decide whether the job and organization fit you. Here are some resources you can go to for information:

- People in your network
- People who work for the company where you will be interviewing
- Job postings
- Company brochures
- Other people who do business with the company
- Reference materials and periodicals in your school or public library

Practicing the Interview

 Tip You must be able to communicate your skills and abilities to an employer. If you can't, you probably will not get the job. Practice can help.

You must be able to communicate your skills and abilities to an employer. If you can't, you probably will not get the job. Practice can help. Many employers ask standard questions in an interview. The questions generally fall into a few categories such as

- Work history and experience
- Strengths and weaknesses
- Goals
- Education or training history
- How you fit the job and the organization

Many books and other publications contain lists of questions that are frequently asked at interviews. Find a list and practice answering the questions. Spend more time on the ones that seem hard to answer. Sometimes schools, colleges or universities, or job-training agencies have workshops on interviewing.

Here are some additional tips to remember:

- Arrive at the interview early.
- Know what is in your resume.
- Bring an extra copy of your resume.
- Think about how you can benefit the company.
- Go into the interview with a positive attitude.
- Give complete but concise answers to questions.
- Do not make negative comments about previous employers.
- Keep your remarks focused on the job.
- Leave personal concerns at home.
- Let the employer bring up salary and compensation.

The questions on the following worksheet are ones employers frequently ask. Get ready for your next interview by answering these questions. If you have completed the other worksheets in this book, you should be able to answer these questions.

Write the answers on the worksheet or record them on an audio- or videotape. Practice in front of a mirror or with a friend who will give you good advice. If you can, find someone who has hiring and interviewing experience. This person can tell you what you're doing right and where you could improve.

The questions in the worksheet are ones an employer might ask you. Record what you would say in response to each question.

My Practice Interview Questions

Employer's Question

My Answer

1. Tell me something about yourself.

1. _____

2. Why are you interested in this job?

2. _____

3. What kind of work have you done before?

3. _____

4. What would previous employers say about you?

4. _____

5. What are your strongest skills and how have you used them?

5. _____

6. What are your weaknesses and what would you like to improve about yourself?

6. _____

7. What have you learned from previous jobs?

7. _____

8. What is your most significant work experience?

8. _____

9. Why should I hire you for this job?

9. _____

Follow-Up

Many employers say that the way a person searches for work tells them what kind of an employee the person will be. Employers would rather give the job to someone who really wants it than to someone who does not seem to care. Follow up after making a contact or having an interview. This shows the employer how eager you are to get the job.

> Employers would rather give the job to someone who really wants it than to someone who does not seem to care.

Consider the following:

- You may be the only applicant who takes the time to write a follow-up letter or make a phone call.

- Your follow-up is an opportunity to tell the employer something you may have forgotten to mention in the interview.

- The employer may have several job openings. If you are not right for one, you may be right for another. Your follow-up gives the employer a reason to take another look at you.

- If the employer is not interested in you, always ask for the name of someone else you can contact for job leads. This will give you power and hope and may lead you to your next job.

- Always follow up within 24–48 hours after the interview.

Job Offers

Looking for work is difficult. Make your decisions carefully. Getting an offer does not necessarily mean you should take the job. Most employers will not expect you to make a decision on the spot. You will probably be given a week or more to make up your mind. Weigh the advantages and disadvantages of the job. Make an informed decision.

> Getting an offer does not necessarily mean you should take the job. Most employers will not expect you to make a decision on the spot.

Evaluating Job Offers

Consider these questions after you get a job offer:

- Do the employer's values match your own?

- What was your initial impression of the company and its employees?

- Did the employees you met seem like people you would want to work with?

- Do the employees seem interested and excited about their work?

Refer to the "My Career Values" (page 34) and "My Life Values" (page 35) worksheets in Chapter 3. Also refer to the "My Perfect Job" worksheet (page 72) in Chapter 5. Use the information in those worksheets to complete the following worksheet. Base your responses on information you gained at the interview.

Carefully consider any job you are offered. Complete the following worksheet. Check the aspects of this position that would match or come close to your idea of the perfect job.

I Evaluate a Job Offer

The Job

_____ Duties and responsibilities

_____ Values/interests/skills

_____ Personalities of supervisors and colleagues

_____ Variety of work assignments

_____ Opportunity for individual achievement

_____ Exposure to outstanding coworkers

_____ Opportunity to work independently

_____ Opportunity and frequency of travel

_____ Overtime

_____ Opportunity to apply academic background

_____ Social significance of job

_____ Physical environment and working conditions

_____ Pressure and pace of work; turnover

_____ Intellectual stimulation

The Organization

_____ Technology used

_____ Management style

_____ Opportunities for growth and advancement

_____ Layoffs and restructuring

_____ Reputation and image of employer

_____ Financial stability and growth prospects

_____ Salary and benefits

_____ People in top-level positions

_____ Personnel policies and flex-time

_____ Training and continuing education

_____ Required relocations and transfers

_____ Public or private employer

_____ Well-established company

The Industry

_____ Growth

_____ Future needs for goods and services

_____ Dependence on government policies and programs

_____ Dependence on the business cycle

_____ Long-term future potential

_____ Record of layoffs or downsizing

The Location

_____ Close to schools

_____ Climate

_____ Cost of living

_____ Community life and environment

_____ Location of company headquarters and branches

Three Job-Offer Options

Imagine that you have interviewed for a job and received a job offer. You can respond in various ways. Here are three options. You can

1. **Reject the offer.** Express your appreciation for the offer and for the company's confidence in you. Say something positive about the employer. Be diplomatic. Send a follow-up letter even if you have already expressed your appreciation verbally.

> You can respond to a job offer by rejecting the offer, by stalling, or by accepting the offer.

2. **Stall.** Express appreciation for the offer. Tell the employer that because this is such an important decision you will need time to think about your decision carefully. Agree on a reasonable time frame for when you will make a final decision. Fortunately, most organizations will not expect you to accept an offer on the spot.

   If you decide to make a counter offer, you only have one chance to do so. Know what you will do if the employer is not open to the terms of your offer. You can ask for what you want, but be prepared for the employer to say no.

3. **Accept the offer.** Show your appreciation for the offer. Ask the employer to confirm the offer in writing. Do not interview for any other positions. Reject all other offers by telephone and then with a short letter. Never go back on an offer you have already accepted.

An Action Checklist

Use the following checklist to keep track of what you have done so far and what you still need to do. You probably already know how to do many of the actions listed in the worksheet. For each action, fill in a target date. Check off each action as you complete it.

My Action Checklist

I will take the following actions to help me look for a job.

Action	Target Date	Completed
Contact employers, colleagues, and other persons. Ask them to serve as references for me.		
Get letters of recommendation from my references.		
Talk with friends, family, business contacts, and other people to discuss job opportunities.		
Update or prepare my resume.		
Prepare a sample cover letter.		
Plan how I will get to the employment interviews and job sites.		
Develop a telephone script.		
Call or write potential employers.		
Send letters and resumes to potential employers.		
Research employers with whom I want to interview.		
Practice my interviewing skills with friends, family, and other contacts.		
Maintain an active file on contacts.		
Follow up interviews with thank-you letters, telephone contacts, and other personal information.		

Some important things I need to remember as I look
for a job:

_____

_____

_____

_____

Keep Your New Job

All the work you have done so far has been in an effort to find the job you want. So what do you need to do after you get the job? The first few days on the job are referred to as a honeymoon. This is because the employer is pleased to have you working. And the employer does not yet expect you to know much about where you will work and what you will do.

Your first week on the job is a good time to demonstrate and begin to document your success on the job. It is a good time to show your interest in how the organization works. It is a good time to get to know your supervisor and coworkers. Use the first few days on the job to learn as much as you can. Don't be afraid to ask questions. Most new workers do not ask enough questions at the beginning and ask too many later on.

Update your resume during your first week on the job. Think about your long-term career plan. Make yourself visible. Create a backup plan for what you will do if aspects of the job do not meet your expectations. The survival of an organization depends in great part on the quality of its workforce. To keep your job you must be successful in the following areas:

1. **Dependability and reliability.** Frequent absences are cause for dismissal. So are absences without good reasons. Employers rely on workers to follow through on their duties.

2. **Punctuality.** Employers expect their employees to report to work on time. Workers who are late at the start of work, late for meetings, or late returning from lunch or breaks cause problems and delay the work of others.

3. **Quality of work.** Employers depend on workers to produce quality products or services. Good quality is important in competing with other organizations. It is a key to company and job survival.

4. **Quantity of work.** Employers are also interested in how much work an employee does. A successful worker produces more than enough goods or services to justify the money he or she makes. A successful worker keeps costs down so the company can make a profit.

5. **Interpersonal communication skills.** Employers do not want employees who cannot get along with their coworkers. An employee who causes problems puts the whole company at risk. So does the employee who does not treat fellow employees with respect and maturity.

Keep these five attributes in mind when you start a new job. Refer to them throughout your career. This will help make you a quality employee.

The following worksheet lists areas you should explore in the first week of your new job. Most of the information here can be provided by your supervisor. Remember to ask questions. Don't guess!

My First-Week Checklist

The checked items indicate what I've learned during the first week on my new job.

Schedule

_____ The hours I work _____

_____ When I can take lunch _____

_____ When I can take breaks _____

_____ How long I have for lunch and for breaks _____

Organizational Structure

_____ Name of my supervisor's boss _____

_____ My supervisor's name _____

_____ My coworkers' names _____

Pay

_____ How often I get paid _____

_____ When pay day is _____

_____ How I will get paid _____

_____ My benefits _____

Job

_____ My job description _____

_____ Details about what I do _____

_____ My work area _____

_____ How my job fits into the overall operation _____

_____ Who to ask when I have questions _____

_____ How I will be evaluated _____

_____ When I will be evaluated _____

_____ Who will evaluate me _____

Policies

_____ Who to call if I'm going to be absent _____

_____ That person's number _____

_____ What happens if I am late _____

_____ How the company ensures security and confidentiality _____

_____ The rules about smoking _____

_____ Where I should park _____

Growing on the Job

If you plan to work, you will have to keep learning and growing. Employers are very careful about who they hire, who they keep, and who they promote. You will be a more valuable asset to your employer if you keep learning new skills. You will also be happier with yourself.

> You will be a more valuable asset to your employer if you keep learning new skills. You will also be happier with yourself.

Employers agree that employees should

- **Know how to learn.** Realize the importance of career-long learning. Take advantage of on-the-job or after-work training.

- **Be able to read, write, and do math.** Improve these skills. They are critical to learning new job duties.

- **Listen and communicate well.** Understand instructions and problems. Communicate effectively with coworkers, supervisors, and customers.

- **Be flexible.** Adapt to changes in technology and in the job. Solve problems creatively. Try new ideas and methods.

- **Be willing to work as part of a team.** Work effectively with others. Be a leader when you need to be. Work with people whose gender, age, race, or cultural background is different than yours.

- **Provide outstanding customer service.** Look for ways to improve relationships with customers and vendors.

- **Have good self-management skills.** Be a self-starter. Be honest and ethical. Take responsibility for your actions. Look for ways to develop and improve skills and traits that are important to the job.

- **Be able to solve problems and think critically.** Always look at the root of the problem. Think about how you can improve the organization.

As you look at the characteristics included in the previous list, compare them to the skills you have. Review the worksheets you completed in Chapter 4. Ask yourself these questions:

- Do I have the skills needed to succeed in my job?

- Which skills can I improve?

- What actions can I take to improve my skills?

Read each statement in the first column of the following worksheet. In the next two columns, check the items you have done or are doing now and the items you will do in the future. Commit yourself to doing those things you need to do. You don't have to do everything on the checklist at once. Refer to it regularly to review the areas in which you can grow.

My Areas for Growth

	I have done or am doing this	I commit myself to doing this in the future
I honestly evaluate the quality and quantity of my work.	_____	_____
I follow through with assignments.	_____	_____
I am on time and reliable.	_____	_____
I show a positive attitude on the job.	_____	_____
I ask for feedback from my supervisor.	_____	_____
I accept feedback from customers and coworkers.	_____	_____
I set my own goals or ask my supervisor to help me.	_____	_____
When evaluated, I try to identify ways I can grow.	_____	_____
I let my supervisor know what I have accomplished.	_____	_____
I take advantage of training the company offers.	_____	_____
I sometimes get training on my own time.	_____	_____
I get involved with classes the company pays for.	_____	_____
I use the company's tuition reimbursement programs.	_____	_____
I volunteer for new assignments, especially if they involve learning new skills.	_____	_____
I volunteer for more responsibility.	_____	_____

Evaluate Your Progress and Modify Your Plan

Tip Don't lose sight of your goals. Make your decisions work for you.

By working through the worksheets in this book, you have completed seven of the eight steps in the Career Decision-Making Model shown on page 86. The eighth and final step is to *evaluate your progress and modify your plan.*

> *"Make no little plans; they have no magic to stir men's blood and probably themselves will not be realized. Make big plans; aim high in hope and work."*
>
> —Daniel H. Burnham

As you evaluate your progress, you may find you are right on track. Or you may discover that something has changed. You may need to set a new goal. Or you may need to change the steps necessary to reach your goal. Remember that the plan and the decisions are yours. You can evaluate and change them anytime.

Look again at the Career Decision-Making Model (page 86). If you need to review any of the steps, do so. Don't lose sight of your goals. Make your decisions work for you. Start over on the decision-making model using new information if you need to.

My Plan Is in Progress

What new pieces of information do I have about the career I decided to pursue? _____

_____

_____

Does this new information change my decision? In what way? _____

_____

_____

Have I reached my goal? If not, what is keeping me from progressing? _____

_____

_____

If I have reached my goal, am I ready to think about a new goal and start the decision-making process again? _____

_____

I will evaluate my progress again on the following date: _____

Ten Keys to Success

Here's a final thought. Memorize the words below. Each begins with one of the letters in the sentence "I do it right." Ten keys to success are

- **I**ntegrity. This means always being honest. Stand by your principles. Don't change your beliefs to fit the situation.

- **D**etermination. This means making up your mind to be successful. Believe that you will be successful. Don't allow anything to stand in your way.

- **O**penness. This means accepting the possibility that ideas can come from anyone or anywhere. Be open to people, ideas, and situations.

- **I**nitiative. This means acting independently when necessary. Make a plan and begin working on it. Revise and change it as needed. Don't wait until your plan is perfect—it never will be.

- **T**ime management. This means that you work on what is most important rather than on what is most pressing.

- **R**esilience. This means getting back up when setbacks knock you down. Everyone fails sometime. Don't allow challenges to stop you or blur your vision of success. In the face of apparent failure, plan again. Revise and adjust as required. Recommit to your vision. Reaffirm your self-confidence.

- **I**magination. This means seeing the future in advance. Don't be afraid to ask questions such as, "Why not?" and "What if?" Many successes come from seeing an old idea in a new way.

- **G**ratitude. This means actively thanking other people. Say thank-you whenever someone is generous or kind. Pass on to others the same help you received.

- **H**umility. This means recognizing that success usually comes when people have worked hard and cooperated. Success is seldom the product of just one person's actions.

- **T**hinking of others first. This means using your abilities to benefit people you have contact with. Find a way to serve others.

WHAT'S NEXT?

Congratulations, you have completed this workbook. In this chapter, you got information you will need when you apply for a job. You considered some ideas for making sure you keep your job.

The next step is to use your portfolio in educational or career interviews. The skills you learn now will be effective throughout your career. Be persistent, committed, positive, and upbeat.

Best wishes to you as you begin your career and job search.